SALT IN MY LIFE

Salt in My Life

poetry

Chinese • English

我生命裡的鹽

英漢雙語詩集

Lien Chao

趙廉

MAWENZI HOUSE

We acknowledge the support of the Canada Council for the Arts for our publishing program. We also acknowledge support from the Government of Ontario through the Ontario Arts Council.

ONTARIO ARTS COUNCIL
CONSEIL DES ARTS DE L'ONTARIO
an Ontario government agency
un organisme du gouvernement de l'Ontario

Canada Council for the Arts | Conseil des arts du Canada

Cover design by Henry Ho and Esther Wong

Library and Archives Canada Cataloguing in Publication

Title: Salt in my life : poetry / Lien Chao = Wo sheng ming li de yan : Ying Han shuang yuan shi ji / Zhao Lian.
Other titles: Wo sheng ming li de yan
Names: Chao, Lien, 1950- author.
Description: Bilingual poetry in English and Chinese.
Identifiers: Canadiana (print) 20190196602 | Canadiana (ebook) 20190197013 | ISBN 9781774150016 (softcover) | ISBN 9781774150023 (HTML) | ISBN 9781774150030 (PDF)
Classification: LCC PS8555.H3955 S25 2019 | DDC C811/.54—dc23

Printed and bound in Canada by Coach House Printing

Mawenzi House Publishers Ltd.
39 Woburn Avenue (B)
Toronto, Ontario M5M 1K5
Canada

www.mawenzihouse.com

In memory of my parents, Liubo Hu and Xianjing Chao; my dearest friend and mentor, Virginia J Rock; my loving sisters Ming and Yun.

I dedicate this book to my family members and my friends, and especially to my grandson, Harry Haynes Chao, born in the morning of a colourful Canadian autumn day, September 25, 2019.

懷念我的父母親，趙賢經和胡柳波；我的摯友和人生導師弗吉尼亞·洛克；和我親愛的妹妹趙明和趙耘。

這本詩集獻給我的家人和朋友們，尤其是我的外孫兒趙曉岩，他於二零一九年九月二十五日早晨誕辰在加拿大這個五彩繽紛的秋天。

Contents

目錄

1. 大地空靈曲：清明，重返華寶山 1
Silence of the Wild Land: Qing Ming, Homebound for Mt. *Hua Bao*
- 一條蜿蜒的路 33
  Along a Zigzagging Path

2. 夕陽大道上的絕唱
Swan Songs on the Sunset Boulevard
- 老爸的反思 36/37
  Old Father's Reflection
- 陪老爸散步 38/39
  Walking with My Aged Father
- 子夜的黑暗 40/41
  Midnight Darkness
- 我是你的最後一根救命稻草！ 42/43
  I Am Your Last Straw!
- 向死而生？ 48/49
  Towards Death, Do We Live?
- 讓岩石飛吧 50/51
  Let the Rock Fly
- 響亮的心跳 52/53
  Palpitating Heartbeats

3. 回形針的歌
Song of the Paperclips
- 閣樓上的灰塵 56-57
  Attic Dusts
- 清除閣樓上的灰塵 58/59
  Cleaning up the Attic Dusts
- 困惑的基本問題 60/61
  Puzzling Questions Starting with A
- 首次去法庭聽會 62-63
  Attending the First Court Conference
- 回形針的歌 64-65
  Song of the Paperclips

4. 沙灘上的卵石
A Pebble on the Beach
- 清晨屬于大海 70/71
  Morning Belongs to the Ocean
- 沙灘上的卵石 72/73
  A Pebble on the Beach
- 三葉草 74/75
  Shamrocks
- 我是一顆星 76/77
  Call Me A Star
- 樹上的蘋果 78/79
  Apple on the Tree
- 小海鷗和蓮蓬籽 80/81
  Kittiwakes and Lotus Seeds

5. 希望之歌
Song of Hope
- 難民申請人 84/85
  A Refugee Claimant
- 難民申請人入冷宮 86/87
  A Refugee Claimant in Limbo
- 不容剝奪的權利 90/91
  Inalienable Rights
- 希望之歌 94/95
  Song of Hope

6. 此時此地
Here and Now
- 雨夜即興亨利家 98/99
  Improvisation at Henry's Home on a Rainy Night
- 奔馳的太極馬 102/103
  Galloping Taiji Horses
- 我生命裡的鹽 106/107
  Salt in My Life

7. 喚醒我們心中的土地 112/113
Awakening the Land within Us

8. 跋：融合 130/131
Epilogue: Fusion

Silence of the Wild Land: Qing Ming, Homebound for Mt. Hua Bao

A Narrative Long Poem

大地空靈曲：清明，重返華寶山

散文體長詩

At the end of the turbulent Proletarian Cultural Revolution (1966-1976), seventeen millions of urban high school students in China were sent to the countryside or remote state-owned farms to be re-educated by peasants through physical labour. Officially, they were given a collective name—the Educated Youth. I was one of those millions.

Forty-five years later, in the spring of 2014, with fellow Educated Youth, schoolmates from Wuhan #2 High School, I took a trip back to our tiny village named Six-Tiled Roofs, situated at the foot of Mount Hua Bao, Tang County, in northern Hubei Province, Central China.

在那場無產階級文化大革命（1966-1976）的浩劫進入尾聲階段，一千七百萬尚未畢業的中國大陸城鎮中學生，被有組織地送往偏遠的農村或國營農場，從事體力勞動，“接受貧下中農再教育。”他們曾經被賦予過一個群體性的名字——知青。我曾經是成千上萬知青中的一員。

2014年春，在告別知青時代四十五年後，我和武漢二中曾經一起插隊的幾位知青，返回鄂北唐縣鎮華寶山腳下那個鮮為人知，當年名叫“六間瓦屋”的小村落。

I. Prologue

Qing Ming Festival
once a year in April
an ancient Chinese tradition
to sweep the ancestors' tombs

each spring
millions of Chinese
on the homebound road
to cemeteries,
to burial grounds,
to the countryside,
to be rejuvenated.

一. 開篇

清明時節
每逢四月
古老傳統
掃墓祭奠

回到祖籍
緬懷先賢
祈福求安
薪火相傳

二. 一張四十五年前的黑白照片

我們一行五人
花甲之年的男女
駕著機動車
融入了
首尾相接的車流
向著鄂北，蜿蜒前行

呼吸著
尾氣瀰漫的空氣
思緒
沿著時間的軌跡
逆行
去追溯
青蔥歲月
似水流年

搜尋著
模糊的記憶
一張退了色的黑白照片
攝於四十五年前：

一個巴掌大的小村莊
名叫六間瓦屋
八個年輕人
好像同胞兄妹
有一個共同的名字——知青

照片上，他們站在
白雪覆蓋的山頂
陽光裡，矯健的身影
雪地上，新鮮的腳印

今天，春風拂面
四十五年前的知青
我們回來了！
迎著曙光
朝露沾濕了
腳上的運動鞋

2. *A black-and-white photo taken forty-five years ago*

Five of us
sixty-some years in age
get into the car
merging with the traffic
bumper to bumper
nudging forward

inhaling engine exhaust
thick and smoky
we let our memories
slow down, wading
backwards to tread
on what remains—
our adolescence
in the thinning matrix
of the bygones.

We start searching, searching for
what's already faded
in a black-and-white photo
taken forty-five years ago:
the contour of a tiny village
named Six-Tiled Roofs
eight teenagers
like brothers and sisters
lived under one roof, sharing
a collective name—
Educated Youth.

In the photo
they stood atop a hill, casting
long shadows behind them,
fresh footsteps
on the deep snow.

Today, in twilight
riding a spring breeze,
the Educated Youth
of forty-five years ago—
we are coming home!
Morning dew wetting the toes
of our athletic shoes.

三. 不見了，昔日的景色

四小時的高速車程
我們進入了唐縣鎮

眼前
一條鄉間車道
不寬不窄
修得堅實平坦
引領我們前行
沿著田邊地頭
繞過堰塘山坡

啊，不見了
黃土飛揚的公路
一道道土坎
拖拉機碾壓下
高低不平的
車轍

不見了
公路上
緩緩穿行的牛群
太陽暴晒下
遺灑在路上的糞團
熱氣蒸騰
瀰漫著
發酵的酸味

不見了
漫山遍野的荊棘灌木
野兔、狐狸、地鼠的出沒
還有，報春的布穀鳥，
啼鳴的黃鸝，
騷動的小山雀

3. Disappearing past landscapes

Four hours on the Highway
we enter Tang County—
under the wheels
a smooth concrete road
neither wide, nor narrow
winding around the fields
up and down the hills

disappeared—
the narrow dirt roads
bumpy and dusty
deeply rutted tracks,
entangled,
made by tractors
carrying heavy loads

disappeared—
passing cows and cattle
piles of cow dung
along the dirt roads
steaming hot in the sun
spreading the sour smell
of fermentation

disappeared—
from the hillside
tangled vines
dusty bushes
hares and weasels
cuckoos in the spring fields
singing birds on high branches
and stirring sparrows

四. 漸行漸遠的農耕文化

田邊的樹籬
高高低低
遮不住我們的視野
彎彎曲曲的田埂
連不成一條直線
油菜花開了
鮮黃鮮黃的
像一張巨大的地毯
浮蓋在田野上

不見了——公路上
肩挑背馱的漢子們
沉甸甸的扁擔
有節奏地顫動
挑擔的人
揮汗如雨
左、右、左、右、左、右
堅實的腳步
踏著音樂的鼓點

不見了——莊稼地裡
嘰嘰喳喳的婦女
播種、除草
年輕的母親們
背著嬰兒下地
談笑風生
休息的哨聲響了
她們撩起衣襟
裸露豐滿的乳房
嬰兒大口地吸吮
母親哼著搖籃曲

不見了——
手握鋤把的青年
祖輩務農
面朝黃土背朝天
不再是他們的宿命
不願意去承傳

4. Disappearing rural culture

Hedges tall and short
can't block our view—
fields zigzagging,
without a straight line
canola blossoms
bright yellow
a vast carpet
floating over
the green fields

disappeared—
male peasants
on the road
carrying heavy loads
with bamboo shoulder poles
swinging
left and right,
left and right,
stepping to drumbeats
sweat dripping down
onto the ground

disappeared—
women in the fields—
seeding weeding
laughing gossiping
young mothers
babies on their backs
in cloth wraps,
when the whistle blew for break
on the edges of the fields
the mothers pulled out their breasts,
to feed the babies
humming lullabies

also disappeared—
teenagers in the fields
a rural heritage
the farming tradition
no longer idealized

五. 華寶山，我們回來了！

那些年
我們結伴進城
天不亮出發
踏著月光回村
來回六十里路
一步一步地
用腳丈量

如今
車輪轉動
丘陵變平川
車外景色躍動
曾經的距離
不再遙遠

山坡上，野火點點
粗心的祭祖人，留下
尚未熄滅的灰燼
風，輕輕地掠過
藍色的火舌舔舐著
像美杜莎頭上的一窩蛇
在那裡搖曳舞動
吞噬枯草
垃圾袋

忽然，一道山梁
出現在地平線上

"華一寶一山!"
我們齊聲呼喊
好像中了彩

啊，高聳的華寶山
我們生命中的喜馬拉雅
我們回來了！

5. Mt Hua Bao, we are coming home!

Remember—
forty-five years ago,
we took the same road to the county
leaving the village at dawn
returning in the moonlight
sixty kilometres on foot
step by step

today
with wheels spinning
hills become flat
sceneries move backwards
shortening the distance

here and there
on the hillside
swirls of smoke
sparks of wildfire
left behind carelessly
by tomb sweepers

the wind blowing across
neglected flames
like a bundle of hissing snakes
their blue tongues
licking dry weeds
devouring
garbage bags

suddenly, in the horizon
a ridge of mountains
looming

"Hua-Bao-Shan!"
we cry out in unison
as if winning a prize

Lofty Mt Hua Bao—
the Himalayas of our lives—
"We are coming home!"

六. 想起一條山澗

拐子們[1]，抬頭看！
前面就是華寶山！

記得嗎
當年，為了燒火做飯
男生們進山買柴
每次每人兩大捆
一根扁擔挑下山
搖搖晃晃十幾里路
上山下山一整天

山路彎彎
山泉淙淙
拐子們擔柴
沿著山路， 一步一步往下走
石頭縫裡聽音樂，水滴石穿
汗水淋漓洗個臉，暢飲清泉

回憶往事
無比感慨
四十五年前
那個奇葩的時代
中國人竟然不懂經濟！
身為世界人口之最國
全體國民被迫勒緊褲帶
為了主義和效忠
成為虔誠的宗教徒

---

1 湖北方言，大哥叫拐子。

6. Remembering a mountain brook

Heads up, Brothers,
I call out aloud:
—Mt Hua Bao—
before our eyes!

Remember—
forty-five years ago
guys buying firewood
in the deep Hua Bao Shan
for our students' home

each of you, each time,
carried two large bundles
one at each end
of a bamboo shoulder pole
swinging and staggering,
step by step, on a ragged footpath
stretching ten kilometres
alongside a mountain brook
gurgling downhill

listening to the stream
quenching your thirst
washing your sweaty faces
with cooling mountain dew.

Reminiscing about
forty-five years ago
what a weird time!
Chinese didn't know economy!
With the largest population
we were forced to tighten our belts
for political loyalty and all the isms—
an entire nation of
religious devotees

七． 到了黃鬍子灣

駛進了一個村落
大拐子停下車
“前面就是黃鬍子灣了！”
他十分肯定地說

路邊過來兩個婦女
身著紅條子工作服

“這裡可是黃鬍子灣?”
“正是！正是！”婦女回答

我驚詫不已
不禁自語
“誰是黃鬍子？
哪裡有個灣?”

拐子們聳聳肩
“這裡沒有水源
為什麼取名灣?”

村頭，路邊
一頭老水牛臥在地上
一條牛繩，拴著
光禿禿的柳樹樁

一座座簡樸的農舍
沒有高牆深院
只有青瓦、紅磚
一台台太陽能熱水器
在屋頂上閃亮
隨意牽接的電線
在風中搖晃
彷彿百足蜈蚣
爬進了蜘蛛網

“陳會計還在世嗎?”
二拐子關切地問
“聽爺爺奶奶說起過，
還有城裡來的知青。 ”

7. Arriving at the Yellow-beard Bay

Entering a village
Elder Brother stops the car,
"This must be Yellow Beard Bay!"
He sounds confident

Two local women walk by
dressed in overalls with red stripes.
"Is this Yellow Beard Bay?"
asks Second Brother
"Yes, it is!"
My jaw drops,
I can't stop mumbling,
"Who is the Yellow Beard?
Why is the village called Bay?"

Guys shrug their shoulders.
"There is no water here,
wondering why,
it's called 'Bay'."

At the head of the village
an old water buffalo, sitting
on the ground, tied
to a leafless willow trunk.

In the village,
no fenced gardens
no wooden gates
all red-brick houses
under black roof tiles.

On top of the roofs
solar water heaters
wires and tubes entangled,
like centipedes' feet caught in spider webs.

"Is Accountant Chen still around?"
asks Elder Brother, excitedly.

"Heard grandparents talk about him,
and Educated Youth from the city,"
answers the middle-aged woman

三拐子摸著滿頭的白髮
感慨地對我說
“四十五年前,
我剛十九歲, 你十七,
他們還沒出世呢。 ”

啊, 捉弄人的時光
驀然間, 我們這些
紅旗下出生的一代人
已經步入了暮年

文化革命
十年政亂
校園被關閉
我們被迫停學
理想徹底破滅

後來毛主席揮揮手:
“知識青年到農村去”
國家有難, 匹夫有責

歷史的悲劇啊
又是我們這一代人
被迫吞下了這顆苦果
簽下一個個盲約
被打發了

我們八個人
落戶華寶山腳下

歲月不饒人那!
三拐子感慨萬千
如今, 我們年過花甲
白髮多過黑髮
去年他中風了
從此老年病痛纏身
我的胞妹明也曾落戶華寶山下
去年癌症奪去她寶貴的生命
有生之年, 誰能忘記
青春少年曾經作為替罪羊
被迫流放

Third Brother strokes his grey hair.
"Forty-five years ago, I was nineteen
you were only seventeen,
they were not born yet."

How time teases!
Our generation
born under the red flag
now seniors.

Remember—
the Cultural Revolution
the political turmoil
lasted more than a decade
schools shut down
societal unrest
our dreams destroyed.

Later, Chairman Mao waved his hand,
"Educated Youth, go to the countryside . . ."
Our nation was in trouble
And the citizens were responsive.

Another tragedy in Chinese history
for our generation to experience,
forced to swallow the bitter fruit
to sign blind dates,
then off to the foot of Mt Hua Bao,
eight of us.

How time flies—
Third Brother exclaims
now that we are in our sixties
with more grey hair than black
he had a stroke last year
suffering a degenerative disease

My sister Ming, also an Educated Youth,
settled at the foot of Hua Bao Shan
lost her battle against ovarian cancer in 2013.
None of us will forget—
those youthful years,
sent away as scapegoats
into exile.

八. 想起了六間瓦屋

還記得嗎
當年的六間瓦屋
除了我們八個知青
還住著貧農郭家兩弟兄，
外加一個老地主
帶著他的孫兒孫女

知青、貧農、地主
左鄰右舍，相安無事
“但是——”大隊支書說
“不准你們和敵人一團和氣”

他天天晚上登門
來講階級鬥爭
“警惕階級敵人
復辟資本主義。”

如今
貧農和地主都已死去
我情不自禁地問
在天堂或者地獄
他們是敵還是友？
是否相逢一笑泯恩仇？

8. Remembering Six-Tiled Roofs

Remember
in our tiny village—
Six-Tiled Roofs—
once lived two brothers named Guo
eight Educated Youth, and
an old landlord with grandchildren

we lived in harmony as neighbours
"But," said the brigade Party secretary
"you are forbidden to get along with the enemy!"
He dropped by every evening
to preach class-struggle theory.

"Keep your political vigilance,"
he urged, "to prevent capitalism
from usurping the power from
the proletariat."

Today,
the poor peasants and the landlord
are all dead, I can't help asking,
if they have reconciled
in heaven or hell,
as friends or as foes,
when passing each other?

九.　一位西北婦女的歸宿

登上山頭
昔日的稻場
四面臨風

還記得
夏收和秋收時節
這個稻場上
通宵達旦
燈火明亮
全隊的男勞力一起上陣
個個汗水淋漓
聲聲吆喝響亮
機器的噪音轟鳴
有如重金屬樂隊在演唱
鏗鏘的節奏
重複著主旋律
金燦燦的穀粒
伴著飛揚的稻草麥秸
雨點般地灑落

如今，站在這山頭上
昔日的喧囂歸於沉寂
唯有耳邊的風
嗚嗚地響

不見了
生產隊的工具房
不見了
靜靜佇立的糧倉

眼前
童話般地出現了
一幢紅磚大瓦房
屋前蹲著一條狗
藍眼睛，尖耳朵，灰皮毛
它不是到處可見的土狗
竟然是一條純種哈士奇犬！

9. A northwestern woman found her destination

We walk up the hill
to the threshing ground
of forty-five years ago

remember—
harvest time
in summer and autumn
this threshing ground
lit up like a tennis court

men of the brigade gathered here
staying awake all night. As long as
the threshing machines were roaring,
guys were smacking and spurting,
louder than a heavy metal band on stage.

They were also jugglers, throwing
grain stalks into the air, golden seeds
raining down
upon their sweaty faces.

Today,
atop the hill
silence prevails
no more harvests.

Disappeared—
the brigade's tool shed
and the granary

a grand red-brick house
miraculously stands high
on the threshing ground

in front of the new house
sits a well-groomed dog
blue eyes, grey fur coat,
sharp pointy ears,
not a local dog but
a husky, actually!

一位婦人
黝黑的皮膚
透紅的圓臉
晃動著一對大辮子
走過來——
幫我們解開了
眼前的“童話”之謎

“告別了貧瘠的大西北
我們一家遷移到這裡。
一千元錢買下這個稻場，
蓋了這座紅磚大瓦房。”

“我女兒在廣州工作
每月寄錢回家
還給我買了這隻寵物狗，
它的名字叫PET，說是外國種，
可聽話啦，非常馴服，
每天吃大米飯加豬肉
過來，過來呀，PET”

Towards us,
comes a northern woman
tanned skin with natural blush
a pair of thick braided pigtails
dangling behind her neck

she unwraps the mystery:
"My family migrated here
from the poor northwestern area.
With one thousand *yuan*,
we bought this threshing ground
we built our new family home"

"My daughter works in Guangzhou
she sends money home
she bought a dog for my companion
his name is P-E-T, a foreign breed,
very, very friendly, eats rice and pork,
come here, come here, Pet . . . "

十． 在時間的地界裡，六間瓦屋消失了

“您老可曾聽說過——
一個名叫六間瓦屋的小村落?”
二拐子急切地問

“那裡曾經居住過
姓郭的兩兄弟，
八個城裡來的知青，
還有一個老地主，
帶著孫兒孫女。 ”

西北女人微笑了
揚揚手，示意我們跟她走
進了院門，來到屋後
跟著搖頭擺尾的寵物狗
我們登上一個高地台
去眺望六間瓦屋

女主人，眯著眼
指著前方的黃土坡
“在那兒，在那兒，
就在那兒了——
六間瓦屋。 ”

順著她手指的方向
我們也眯起眼
目不轉睛地
凝視遠方
遠方——
空蕩蕩的一片黃土
坦陳在藍天下
沒有一絲雲彩

“我們的村莊呢？
我們的六間瓦屋——在哪裡？
怎麼看不見了，
難道人間蒸發了，
像海市蜃樓？ ”

10. *Disappeared Six-Tiled Roofs within the boundaries of time*

"Excuse us, have you ever heard about
a village called Six-Tiled Roofs? "
asks Second Brother
almost impatiently.

"There once lived two brothers
with the family name Guo,
eight Educated Youth, and
an old landlord with grandchildren."

The northern woman smiles
makes a hand gesture,
we follow her inside the gate
to the back of her house.

Pet wags its tail,
welcoming the visitors.
We ascend onto a lookout spot
behind the northern woman

raising her right arm
she points firmly ahead,
her eyes squinting
across the vast yellow earth.

"There, there—
over there—Six-Tiled Roofs!"

Following her pointing finger
we also squint our eyes,
staring ahead—
from near to afar
yellow dirt mounds
under the blue sky
not even a shadow of cloud.

"Where is our village,
our Six-Tiled Roofs?"
Can't see it . . .
did it evaporate,
like a mirage?"

西北女人點點頭
“是啊——散了，
散了，都散了！ ”

她的話，如晴天霹靂
砸在我們的頭頂上
失去了感知的能力
我們相視無語

六間瓦屋
我們曾經的住所
我們曾經的村莊

六間瓦屋
一個不起眼的名字
一個珍藏在我們心中
四十五年的
黑白記憶

眼前
不見斷牆殘壁
沒有沙石瓦礫
六間瓦屋的記憶
伴隨我們青春的足跡
還沒來得及講述的故事
在溫暖的春風裡
飄散了

眼前
只有塵土，一層又一層
堆起了一個個黃土坡
像壯闊的波瀾會入大海

塵埃落定
沉積為大地
藍色的天庭下
只有，永久的空靈

The northern woman nods,
Continues to nod and nod,
"Yes, scattered,
all scattered . . . "

Her words
echoing under the blue sky
knocking out our senses,
we are wordless.

Six-Tiled Roofs—
maybe an insignificant name
but it was our home—our village—
we cherished it for forty-five years
a black-and-white memory

before our eyes
neither a collapsed wall
nor a piece of broken tile.

Our memory starts to fade,
dispersing in the warm breeze
with our youthful footprints
our untold stories—

before our eyes
only dust mounds
dust on dust onto the earthy hills
like waves merging into the ocean
earth mixes with the landscape
under the dome of the blue sky,
the eternity of void.

十一. 地界裡的新塚

黃土風塵的地界裡
現出了兩處新築的墳塚
祭祖的人似乎剛剛離去
留下了色彩鮮豔的紙花
一堆尚未燃透的灰燼
幾絲青煙裊裊升起
依依地繞著墓碑
似乎不願散去

二拐子咳了一聲
長長地嘆了口氣
“或許，安息在這墓穴裡的
是大老郭和他的妻子。”

忽然，一陣風起
風裡帶著哨音
猶如一串風鈴，聲聲幽怨
燃盡的紙灰飄散著
像聞聲起舞的灰蝴蝶

此時此刻
此景此情

我們一行五人
彷彿時間穿梭
從四十五年前
那張黑白照片中
走了出來

從只有上帝才知道的地方
我們又出現在這片土地上

在這清明時節
這祭奠的時刻
我們心懷敬畏

茫然
失落
恍惚
頓悟

II. New earthy landmarks

From the dusty monotone earth
appear all of a sudden,
two newly erected landmarks—
freshly attended by tomb-sweepers,
leaving behind colourful paper flowers,
piles of ashes, smothered fire, and
lonely swirls of blue smoke, rising
and hovering around the tombstones.

Second Brother utters
in a deep, guttural voice
"Perhaps—resting inside
the new graves were
Old Guo and his wife."

A gust of dusty wind
blows across
the air whistles, like
a string of wind chimes plucked
a lonesome music, soft to the ear
ashes at the gravesides
flying up like grey butterflies.

The five of us stunned
witnessing
time travelling
we are walking down
from the black-and-white photo
from only God-knows-where
to reappear on this land.

This Qing Ming
we pay our homage
with awe and respect
our stomachs churning
heads spinning
some fuzziness
a momentary reflection
a clearer vision
an affirmation.

十二． 尾聲：回歸

三百六十度，轉了一個圈
黃土坡外，果樹成林

“我把這片山租給了一個果農”
西北女人鄭重地對我們說

“如果你們兩個星期前來就好了，
那時候，山上山下桃花一片！ ”

是啊，如今
繽紛的落英
溶入了黃土
翠綠的葉芽
在枝頭暴突

花開花謝
人來人去

大地
訴說了她的故事
揭示了藍天下的秘密
盡收了所有銘心刻骨的變遷
終究，又回歸到寂寥和安寧

是的，四十五年前
我們曾經來過這裡
今天，我們回來了
我們不虛此行

“照個相吧，”
大嫂建議
舉起了照相機
留下這個清明的記憶

12. Epilogue: Rejuvenation

With a 360-degree spin
we see orchards on the hillside
"I rent out the hill to a fruit farmer,"
declares the northern woman.

"If you came two weeks earlier,
peach blossoms covered the entire hill."
Her smiling face, pink and translucent,
a ripening fruit

and now, all the colourful clouds
have been ingested by the earth
numerous green shoots
budding on the branches.

Flowers bloom, flowers wither,
a generation comes and passes on.

The land has told us her stories,
some mysteries under the blue sky—
after witnessing the incredible
the land returns to peace and serenity.

Yes, we were here forty-five years ago
and today, to this land, we have returned—
to complete perhaps
a worthwhile journey.

"Let's take a picture,"
suggests Elder Brother's wife,
raising her camera
"to honour this trip."

黄昏，落日，晚霞
墓塚，香火，紙花

twilight, sunset, colourful clouds
tombs, ashes, bright paper flowers

起伏連綿的黄土坡
一陣陣的風沙刮過

yellow earthy mounds, merging
and looming, when the wind blows

別了
六間瓦屋

Farewell
Six-Tiled Roofs

再見
華寶山

Good-bye
Mount Hua Bao

Spring 2018
Toronto, Canada

NOTE, In the early winter of 1969, the tiny village named Six-Tiled Roofs received eight Educated Youth sent by Wuhan No. 2 High School. The four male students were Zhao Bigui, Kang Jingguo, Jiang Haisong, and Xin Yongxiang; the four female students were Jiang Haiping, Jia Ke, Chao Lien, and Xie Xin.

附註：公元一九六九年初冬，這個只有六間瓦屋的小村落接受了來自武漢二中的八位知青。 四位男生是趙壁歸、康經國、江海松和辛永祥；四位女生是江海萍、賈可、趙廉和謝欣。

一條蜿蜒的路

Along a zigzagging path

Anxious to preserve our initial response during the trip, I took notes along the way. 二零一四年五月七日起筆創作中文詩稿，改變了我一貫的創作順序，五月二十六日中文初稿完，七月開始英文創作。

Completing the first draft in English on 23 July 2014, my sister Nan's birthday, she was also an Educated Youth. 英文初稿完成於同年七月二十三日，胞妹趙南的生日，她曾經也是一名知青。

Three years after the first draft, I revised the English text in January 2017. 改動了英文就要修改中文，二零一七年的早春二月修改中文稿。

Following the Chinese revision, I updated the English verse again on September 23, 2017, my dear friend Virginia Rock's birthday. It was on her 61 birthday in 1984, I arrived in Canada. She passed away in 2015.

When it's time to invite friends to read the manuscript, my dear friend Patty Rivera, a fellow poet, agrees to read the English version. I printed out half of the manuscript for her. 另一半中文詩稿發給了妹夫徐寅生，詩歌愛好者，他是胞妹趙明的丈夫。明也是知青，曾經落戶華寶山下。

2014年清明，幾位女村民念念不忘明曾經幫助她們購買縫紉機的事，我不忍心告訴她們明已經不在人世了。只能在心裡默默地告慰明的在天之靈　。妹夫寅生對我的中文詩稿提出了寶貴的修改建議。每次修改，我彷彿又一次地俳徊在六間瓦屋消失的天地間。

Every revision took me back to the unforgettable Qing Ming of 2014, to the dusty land under the blue sky, the wind blew with a whistle, where our Six-Tiled Roofs had vanished.

窗外一場大雪正在紛紛揚揚地下著，地面上一片白茫茫。我注視著混沌的世界，車轍和腳印快速地消失在雪景中，今天紀念胞妹趙耘五十五歲生日

2018 年1月31日
我不再等待　。

Another snowfall was covering up the city, adding no significance to the silent wintry night. I gazed at the quiet street under the hazy street light, tracks left by passing vehicles, footprints by a few pedestrians quickly disappeared in the snow, merging with the landscape. Today would have been my sister Yun's fifty-fifth birthday.

For all of you, I waited no longer.
January 31, 2018

Swan Songs on the Sunset Boulevard
夕陽大道上的絕唱

The shadow of the Pagoda tree slants toward
the ground, as if hiding some mysteries
龍爪槐的影子在地面上越來越長
樹蔭裡似乎藏著玄機

老爸的反思

爸問我
“你媽睡在哪裡？”
我給他蓋好棉被，關了燈
道過一聲，“晚安，爸。”

“我媽嘛，”我想說
她去天堂十多年了，
靈魂不睡覺。不過，
爸聽不懂這些故事

我給爸的腿上蓋上毛毯
九十多歲的老人，血脈細緩
他常說腳冷。爸又嘀咕起來
“你媽，她睡在哪裡？”

爸定是進入了夢境
在時光的隧道裡穿行
退行的大腦，模糊的記憶
在現在和過去之間
不時地，有靈光閃現

在那些糾葛的年代裡
父母曾經共享一間臥室
明裡暗裡，他們之間發生了冷戰
床上築了一道隱形的柏林牆
爸不理睬睡在床另一頭的妻子

爸鼾聲如雷，媽多年失眠
有一天，媽走了……
從此，爸獨自在黑夜裡打鼾
有時他深夜醒來，喃喃地喚著媽的名字：
“柳波，你晚上睡在哪裡？”

中文2017年8月21日
Chinese poem August 21, 2017

Old Father's Reflections

Father asks me,
"Where does your mother sleep?"
when I tuck him in bed, switching off
the light, and wishing him good night.

My mother? I want to say—
she has been in heaven for a decade—
the spirit doesn't sleep, but this story
makes no sense to my father.

I cover up his feet with another blanket—
in his nineties, circulation slows down
he has cold feet. Father mumbles again,
"Where does your mother sleep?"

He must be dreaming, or in a state of
reminiscence, maybe time-travelling
to a timeless place, his age-addled brain
erases the gap between present and past, but
from time to time, clarity flares up like a flame.

While entangled in a related place
my parents used to share a bedroom
secretly and openly, a cold war was waged
with an invisible wall in bed, he cared little
about his wife, her pillow placed at the other end.

He snores like thunder discharged, she suffered
her insomnia each night. One day, she passed away,
he snores alone in the darkness ever since. Occasionally,
waking up at night, he utters a heartfelt mumble,
"Liu Bo, where do you sleep at night?"

December 26, 2011
Edited August 8, Oct. 22, 2017

陪老爸散步

一條漫漫的冬日的小路，佇立著
挺拔的枯草，草雖枯黃，卻十分柔韌
在凜冽的寒風中起伏搖晃

年逾九旬的父親推著嶄新的助步車
沿著小路蹣跚挪步，滿口假牙的他，
津津樂道他的四輪驅動，他的新“卡車”

沿著花園小徑，通往夕陽大道
我陪老爸練車，走在他的身旁
直行！急轉彎！走在路中央！

地平線上，一輪夕陽西下
我大聲地提醒父親
當心！慢行！看前方！

路過一棵龍爪槐，老爸在助步車上小坐
傘樹里棲息著無數隻小麻雀，飛進，飛出
棕色的羽毛，白色的圓肚子，嘰嘰喳喳地叫個不停

“麻雀不知道飢餓，才會這麼快樂”
我心不在焉地說。鳥兒們刮躁地歌唱
好像在炫耀它們無憂無慮的麻雀生活

樹蔭下，老爸眼簾低垂，彷彿在沉思
淡淡的笑容浮現時，他說了一句中國成語：
“麻雀雖小，五臟俱全。”

龍爪槐的樹影在地面上越伸越長
樹蔭裡似乎藏著玄機。在夕陽的餘輝裡
我窺視到其中的奧秘：輕鬆地陪老爸散步去

中文2017年8月21日
Chinese poem August 21, 2017

Walking with My Aged Father

A wintry path laced with tall grass,
withered maybe, the grass appears resilient,
bending down, standing up, when the cold wind sweeps

my father, in his nineties, wearing full-set dentures,
shuffles forward, pushing a new walker
joyfully, he chats about his 4x4, his brand new "truck."

Down the garden path, towards a sunset boulevard
Father maneuvers his new truck, with me coaching him
Go straight! A sharp turn! Stay on the path!

On the horizon, the sun is descending fast
I raise my voice, reminding old father
"Watch out!" "Slow down!" "Look up!"

Passing a Chinese Pagoda tree, Father sits down,
watching sparrows with brown feathers and white bellies
darting in and out from under the hanging branches

"Sparrows aren't hungry, so they live happily," I comment
absent-mindedly. Sparrows are noisy, sing aimlessly,
as if to show off, totally worry-free.

Father ponders in the shadow of the umbrella tree, his eyelids
droopy. When a smile appears, he utters an old Chinese saying,
"Sparrows, though small, have the guts of all five organs."

The shadow of the Pagoda tree slants towards the ground,
hiding mysteries. In the vanishing sunbeam, an aperture
reveals the secret to me: walk LEISURELY with old daddy

January 2, 2012
Edited on March 16, 2018

子夜的黑暗

加濕器的噴嘴在旋轉，吐雲吐霧，一圈圈，
粉末般的雪，紛紛揚揚，積累在窗檐

計時的沙漏不斷地傾斜，顫抖的沙粒，源源地
穿孔而下，流逝的時光融入了子夜的黑暗

不肯平靜的大腦拒絕睡意的侵襲
紊亂無序的腦電波沖開了意識的大門

零星的照片、遺失的信件、沒有記錄的談話、
謠言、緋聞、鮮為人知的秘密，不肯壽終正寢

思緒的空間一次次地洗著手裡這把紙牌
東拼西湊，撰寫不出一篇可讀性的家書

我聽見腳步聲由遠而近，然後輕盈地落在
通往我臥室的樓梯上。此刻，聲音從樓下傳來——

那是父親絕望的夢囈，夾雜著他少有的道歉
子夜的黑暗濃縮成又一個不眠之夜的噩夢

晝夜輪轉，夜色漸褪，在黎明將至的時分，我心甘情願地，
再一次選擇了那條早已踏平了的歸途——諒解和寬恕

中文2017年8月21日
Chinese poem August 21, 2017
Edited November 23, 2017

Midnight Darkness

The humidifier sprays a mist from its rotating nozzle
dry snow powder accumulates on the window ledge

an hour-glass tilts, shivering sand is passing through
a tiny hole, silence measures the density of the midnight darkness

the restless brain refuses to settle, wandering thoughts
push through the doors to enter the home of consciousness

a few old photos, lost letters, unrecorded conversations, rumours
and gossip, undisclosed secrets, all fragmented, not entirely muffled

the mind's chamber shuffles the incomplete data like a handful of cards,
piecing them together, this way that way, can't make a cohering saga

I hear ghostly footsteps approaching from afar, landing quietly
on the staircase towards my bedroom, when suddenly, despairing cries

from one floor below, my father mumbles his occasional apologies,
thickening the midnight darkness into another sleepless nightmare

tossing in bed, before night decays into dawn, relenting, I choose
to surrender to the well-trodden family path of remorse and forgiveness

Feb. 13, 2014
Edited August 3, Oct. 22, 2017

我是你的最後一根救命稻草！

你——
躺在那裡
雙目緊閉
被牆一樣嚴實的帷幔隔離
管子從你的嘴裡伸出——
你像龍，長著幾根觸鬚
可是，你是被駕馭的龍，
鏈接在呼吸機上

機器不停地閃爍
發出有節奏的聲響
刻下線條，畫出圖像
護士說機器在給你輸氧
記錄你呼吸的頻率
測出你的肺活量
它讓你的生命得以延續

你的專人護士
坐在你腳的後方
正在填寫一張大表
她像個警惕的衛兵
時刻捍衛著你的財產
而你卻像一根木頭
或者一塊岩石
ROCK正是你的家姓
寂然無聲
全然不予理會

每天來看望你的時候
我像個受驚嚇的孩子
憋著氣，對著牆上的對講機
報出了你和我的姓名
盼望自動門緩緩開啟

I Am Your Last Straw!

You—
lying there,
eyes closed,
surrounded by curtains like walls
tubes sticking out from your mouth
you look like a dragon with a few whiskers
but harnessed
attached to a machine—
a ventilator

The breathing machine
beeps and flickers,
drawing diagrams,
abstract irregular lines,
conveying oxygen, says the nurse,
it measures your breath,
inhaling and exhaling—
a life-support device

Your personal nurse, sitting
at the foot of your bed,
a watchful sentinel
she files a large chart
guarding your property

Your breath is shallow
you look like a log
a piece of Rock
which is your last name
too still, motionless, abnormal

Whenever I come to visit
I am a scared child
holding my breath,
saying my name and yours
through a speaker on the wall
after granting the permission
the automatic door opens

當我輕手輕腳地
走進特護病房的大門時
其他病人家屬，繼續等候著
臉上露出了羡慕的神情

特護病房裡的病人
面如土色
你們沒有姓名
只有床位號碼
不論男女老少
亞裔、非裔，還是歐裔
裹在醫院的病號服裡
個個呼吸艱難
依靠呼吸機

護士們身著灰綠色套裝
和那堵隔離帷幔的顏色一模一樣
有個護士裹著件全身長的護士服
好像穿著日本和服，邁著碎步
不知她是無心還是有意
何必在此標新立異？

走進特護病房
我的心上壓著鉛
舌頭朝後曲卷
我不斷地吞口水
給自己壯膽
我的眼皮顫抖
卻無法辨別是左還是右
大腦裡一片空白
我只記得Joe Vitale說過
在最危急的情況下，
啟用夏威夷土著人的密咒
是求助希望的最後一根稻草
O'hou lopolo
I love you
I love you

into the MSICU, gingerly
I enter on tiptoes, while
relatives of other patients
in the waiting-room,
look envious

Inside the MSICU
beds are numbered without names
all of you, grey and silent,
young and old, male or female
Asian, African, and Caucasian
all wrapped-up in hospital gowns
breath like shadows
attached to ventilators

Nurses wear solid greyish-green colour
matching the separating curtain walls
one female nurse wraps herself up
laboriously, in a long piece of cloth
as if a Japanese kimono
she moves around with tiny steps
being mischievous or not intending
a senseless taste, why look
different in the MSICU?

My heart weighs like lead
my tongue curls backwards
I swallow to stay strong
my eyelids twitching
but I can't tell left or right
I can only remember
Joe Vitale's instruction
to use a native Hawaiian incantation
as a last straw for hope
O'hou lopolo
I love you
I love you

忽然間，我想起了
加拿大國家廣播電台
《白大褂，黑魔術》的節目
護士們告訴我，
你說你受夠了。
她們在暗示我，
是否可以停止治療，
一個住院醫隨聲附和，
“昨晚他們還做了筆錄”
“那麼請給我看她的簽字”
我沒有忘記向他們索取證據

醫生和護士的臉上
露出同情的神色
隔離帷幔，特護病房
昏沉的噪音，使我迷惘
MSICU, MSICU, MSICU,
MSICU, MSICU ……

震驚之餘，我把自己喚醒
我是你的最後一根救命稻草！
緊緊地抓住我，
天還沒有塌下來
O'hou lopolo
I love you
I love you so much
我不放手！

中文2017年8月28日
Chinese poem August 28, 2017

Suddenly, I remember
"White Coat, Black Art"
a CBC Radio Program
Some nurses claim last night
you said you had enough,
indicating they could stop treatment
A resident doctor echoes
"They documented this last night."
"Then show me her signature,"
I ask them for proof

A sympathetic look
reappears on their faces
drowsy noises saddening me,
mesmerizing me, within
the curtained walls

MSICU, MSICU MSICU
MSICU, MSICU . . .

I AM YOUR LAST STRAW!
I shake myself awake
holding on to me now
before the sky falls
O'hou lopolo
I love you
I love you so much—
I WILL NOT LET GO!

First draft May 2015
Finished on July 31, 2017

向死而生？

慟哭、嚎啕、 嘶叫、抽泣
我和明坐進她的汽車裡，
胞妹耘被癌症殘酷折磨，
切膚之痛，撕碎了我們脆弱的心
靈魂的支柱坍塌了

耘，我們的小么妹
小我十三歲，小明九歲，
一個精湛的婦產科專家，
拯救過無數生命，卻無力挽救她自己
不知道我們天生就繼承了變異基因

癌魔改變了她的和顏悅色
她那充滿陽光的愛心田園
變成暴風驟雨施虐的黑夜
憤怒的雷電吐出邪惡的火焰

她心中溫柔的愛
被仇恨的利刃劃開
癌腫的毒液流出來
神經裸露，血跡斑斑

向死而生，全靠愛和希望
難道還有第二條路嗎？
我沒有勇氣向耘重複，目睹了
癌魔用暴力扼殺了她最後的希望

無奈的明，發動了汽車引擎，
噪音是我們撕心裂肺的呼喊。
在沒有月光，沒有午夜鐘聲的北京城，
我們度過了耘最後的聖誕節前夜

中文2017年8月28日
Chinese poem August 28, 2017

Towards Death, Do We Live?

weeping, sobbing, wailing, screaming . . .
Ming and I, back into her car, defeated,
savage cancer strangled Yun's last hope, with
broken hearts, only angst left, our souls caved in

our youngest sister, thirteen years my junior,
nine to Ming. Yun, a renowned gynecologist,
saved many lives, fighting for her own, without
knowing we were born with the bad genes

monstrous cancer, the devil had altered
the gentleness in her colour, a sunshine
person became a stormy hurricane
thunderous rage spitting out sinister fire

tender love was slashed by a sharp blade,
hatred, like poison blood, oozed out,
exposing our vulnerable love, and
sensitive nerves of the same heredity

towards death, we live our lives with
love and hope, is there another way?
But I lost the courage to say this to Yun,
when I saw the cancer do its killing

Ming ignited the engine, the roaring noise was
our hoarse scream. On this icy, moonless night
in Beijing, no bell ringing at midnight, we spent
the last Christmas Eve with Yun

Drafted Dec. 24, 2009
Edited July 31, 2017
August 2, 2017

讓岩石飛吧

一個生命走了，
千變萬化……

讓那塊岩石飛吧，
你無法捧起它的重量

岩石化成了灰燼，
讓風刮起來，帶走所有的包袱……

不再有仇，不再有愛，甚至知識和智慧，
放棄這一切，我們就能飛翔

在塵世的光亮裡， 一隻蝴蝶翩翩起舞
做一隻蝴蝶吧， 朝著正午的陽光飛翔……

這首詩是好友何家強得知弗吉尼亞去世所作 。
他不知道弗吉尼亞姓ROCK，正是“岩石”。
我收到後，十分震撼，一直珍藏 。
它伴隨我度過了痛失摯友
和親人的日子。

中文譯稿：
2017年9月23日

Let the Rock Fly

a life goes,
it will transform . . .

please let the rock go,
which is too heavy to hold

transform the rock into dust,
let the wind blow, blow away all the attachments . . .

no hatred, no love, not even knowledge or wisdom,
with a lighter mind, we can fly

under the beam, within the dust,
dance like a butterfly

be a butterfly,
follow the bright beam at noon

The poem was written by my dear friend Henry Ho upon
the passing of Virginia Rock on November 17, 2015.
Henry didn't know Virginia's last name was Rock.
I immensely appreciated his spiritual insight.
The poem has helped me deal with
losses of beloved friends
and family members.

響亮的心跳

我聽見自己的嘆息聲
不知是平靜還是沮喪
蟄居在四壁圍牆的空間
磚孔石縫裡充滿了記憶

我羡慕會唱歌的人
或者吹個口哨， 哼個小調
廚房的冰箱，也會情不自禁地釋懷
間歇性地，用幾個音符低唱

我渴望聽見開懷的笑聲
在三代人之間傳遞
在晚餐的飯桌上彈跳
當我們一起品嚐英語和漢語的味道

入夜了，我點上蠟燭，和你們
絮叨咱們家的那些故事和人物
閃爍的燭光在我的呼吸裡晃動
我聽見擊鼓般響亮的心跳

中文2017年9月1日
Chinese poem September 1, 2017

Palpitating Heartbeats

I hear myself sigh
for peace and for despair
enclosed within the four walls,
porous bricks permeated with memories

I envy those who can sing or whistle,
at least hum a wordless tune,
even a refrigerator within intervals
bursts out a few musical notes

I long to hear the hearty laughter
among our three generations, bouncing
back and forth on the dinner table
when we were tasting English and Chinese

at night, I light a candle to all of you, so
I can record our family saga and its characters
a single flame flickers within my breath
I hear palpitating heartbeats like drums

February 15, 2013
Edited August 11, 2017

Song of the Paperclips

回形針的歌

I hear Lao Tzu laughing aloud in the thick clouds: All storms in nature start with a good cry, and end, the blue sky.

從烏云密布的天空，傳來了老子爽朗的笑聲：
自然界的一切風暴都以慟哭開始，以藍天告終。

閣樓上的灰塵

眼淚
從何而來?
悲傷
為何而生?

打掃閣樓
記憶如塵埃
十年創作
付之一炬
卻揮之不去

紙片上的文字
曾經的記錄
蹂躪成團
踩在腳底
殘骸遍地

畫筆身首分離
書籍被強暴
書封從書脊被斷裂
沒有留下一頁字跡

忍無可忍
我問四壁
是什麼動機
孕育了仇恨?

垃圾袋
拋出門外
毫不猶豫
隱痛猶存

中文2017年8月22日
Chinese poem August 22, 2017

Attic Dusts

Tears
from where?
sadness
for what?

cleaning up
the attic
dusted by
memories

creativities
a decade long
being savaged, but
can't be dusted off

notes
once scribbled
crumpled up
stepped down

carcasses everywhere
paint brushes
without tips
or tubes

book covers
torn off from the spines
not a page of words
attached

To the bare walls
I can't stop asking
what has motivated
such hatred?

garbage bags
being tossed out
without hesitation
a dull pain remains

October 22, 2011
Edited on August 5, 2017

掃除閣樓上的灰塵

查看《多倫多星報》週末訃告版，沒有找到——
毫不奇怪，誰會為關係破裂登報。人與人之間

磨擦消耗，死亡是最終的出路。一隻蒼蠅的殭屍
懸掛在牆角的蜘蛛網裡，遍體鱗傷，折斷了翅膀。

我相信它是活著飛進了蛛網。暖風帶來智者的勸誡：
應該徹底清除這段往事了，首先和首要的是

慟哭一場。剪斷自我憐憫的情結，
淡出往事，既然悔之已晚，何必懺悔？

瞬間，瓢潑大雨從天而降，鼓點般地撞擊在
玻璃窗上。雷聲裡夾著閃電，轟隆隆地響成一片

從烏云密布的天空，傳來了老子渾然而遙遠的笑聲：
自然界的一切風暴都以慟哭開始，以藍天告終。

中文2017年8月23日
Chinese poem August 23, 2017

Cleaning Up the Attic Dusts

Looking through the obituaries in the weekend *Toronto Star*,
not found, not surprised—who publishes broken relationships?

After wear and tear, death is the way out. Corpse of a fly
hanging in a spider's web, signs of struggle, wings broken.

I am sure it flew in alive. Warm breeze brings words from
a wise friend: Time to start cleansing, first and foremost,

a good cry. Then, sever the emotional ties
too late to regret, no need to repent.

A heavy shower comes down, drumming on the windows
thunder explodes with flashes of lightning

I hear Lao Tzu laughing aloud in the thick clouds: All storms
in nature start with a good cry, and end, the blue sky.

October 24, 2011, Monday, rainy
Edited August 6, Oct. 22, 2017

困惑的基本問題

——寫在第一次去法庭之前

彷彿
走在燃燒的炭火上
皮膚被燒烤
靈魂冷噤

既然
“生存還是毀滅，這是個問題”
還有什麼比“生存”和“毀滅”
更值得考量？

以為
植下一棵發芽的苗
就會長出一片閃光的綠
綻放出璀璨的花朵
卻不知這一株居然是毒草
難道要植樹人自食其果？

都說
善有善報，
惡有惡報 。
善、惡本如油水分離
凡夫俗子，為什麼
不遵循智慧的配方？

中文2017年8月24日
Chinese poem August 24, 2017

Puzzling Questions Starting with A

—Written before the first court conference

As if,
walking on burning charcoal
skin scorched
soul stays cool to observe

"To be or not to be, that is the question,"
what else is noteworthy of
more consideration?

Assume
planting a spouting root
green leaves will grow, then glorious blossoms
but this one turns out with deadly poison
expect the gardener to eat the fruits?

All say
what goes around comes around,
good and evil do not mingle, just like
water and oil. Why didn't the mortals
ever warrant this wise formula?

Early winter, Nov. 2011
Edited August 10, 2017

首次去法院聽證

瘋狂——
像煉獄裡熊熊燃燒的烈火

謊言——
巧舌如簧地從蛀齒的縫隙間洩出

罪惡感——
將視線壓倒在地上

恐懼——
蜷縮在法官咄咄逼人的目光掃不到的角落

法官說——
在這個房間裡，有兩個人知道事情的真相

最後，法官又說——
你們的律師不會提供免費服務

中文2017年8月24日
Chinese poem August 24, 2017

Attending the First Court Conference

insanity—
burns with licking flames from the infernal fire

lies—
passing the slippery tongue to squeeze through crooked teeth

guilt—
weighing down the sight onto the ground

fear—
crouches in the corners to avoid the judge's penetrating gaze

the judge says—
two people in the room knew the factual truth

the judge concludes—
your lawyers will not work for free

December 5, 2011
Edited August 10, 2017

回形針的歌

那天
打掃閣樓
偶見一個
塵封的文件箱
裝滿了牛皮紙信封
沒有上鎖

今天
抹去浮塵
打開箱蓋
倒出全部內容：
昔日的發票收據
好像十年之久
用回形針分開
一疊一疊地
在文件箱底
早已遺忘

想當年
這些發票
光鮮
這些回形針
錚亮
彎曲成兩個環路，
兩端頭藏起來
像女孩子的髮卡

如今，
回形針——
竟令人不堪地
衰老了！

然而，似乎更加執著
完全不肯鬆手
似乎有過一個鄭重的承諾
被初心所束搏

Song of the Paperclips

that day,
cleaning the attic
I moved a filing box
full of brown envelopes
unlocked

today,
dusting the lid
I release the contents:
stacks of receipts
from the envelopes
bundled by paperclips
left inside the filing box
forgotten

a decade ago,
the receipts were
fresh
the paperclips
shiny
two curvy loops
ends tucked in,
like hairpins

now the paperclips
are aged
but determined
resisting to be undone
as if bound by a promise
initially pledged

回形針的鏽斑，像泥濘的腳印
像凝固的血跡，牙咬的齒痕
留在皺褶的紙條上
十分搶眼，
無聲勝有聲

無情的時間，
從薄脆的發票上
抹去了文字、數據、價錢和稅款，
一切有價值的信息資料
在漫長的黑夜裡
消失殆盡

然而，這些回形針
以始終不渝的固執
拒不放手

中文2017年8月25-28日
Chinese poem August 25-28, 2017

leaving rusty marks like footprints,
blood stains, tooth marks
on wrinkled paper
visible and silent
louder than words

ten years,
have mercilessly wiped out
the contents,
figures, prices, taxes
vanished in darkness,
and nothing to be traced

but the rusty paperclips
hold on
in unyielding stubbornness

Drafted April 1, 2015;
Rewritten on August 26, Oct. 22, 2017

A Pebble on the Beach
沙灘上的卵石

Picking up a pebble on the beach,
smooth, stony, and a good grip
在海邊拾起一塊卵石
光滑，石質，握力好

清晨屬於大海

大海從搖蕩的夢中醒來
彎彎曲曲的海岸，潮漲潮落
浪濤演奏著海的樂章，不斷地
改變天空和沙灘之間的情結

沙雀不停地在海灘上留下腳印
彷彿在紀錄大海的樂章，感動目擊者
海水溫情地湧了進來，擦掉腳印
抹平沙灘，彷彿這裡不曾有過任何痕跡

海鷗駕著鹹味的風，聲嘶力竭地
呼叫，開啟了大海一天的喧囂
有些鳥兒一個猛子扎進洶湧的波濤
堅硬的喙，無力改變大海的主旋律

我躍入海的懷抱，雙手為槳
自由自在地漂浮在溫暖的水面上
忽然一個渤湧的浪尖，把我高高地舉起
酣暢淋漓地，讓我品嚐了苦澀有餘的大海

中文2017年8月28日
Chinese poem August 28, 2017

Morning Belongs to the Ocean

Ocean wakes up from a tumbling dream,
seashores zigzagging, tides high and low,
playing an oceanic symphony, transforming
the sphere between the sky and the beach

sandpipers continue to make footprints
notating ocean's music, overwhelming the onlooker
waves push in gently, erasing all the lines, as if
nothing ever happened on the sandy beach

Riding the salty wind, gulls cry aloud, piercing and
screaming, a harsh pitch in the morning symphony,
some birds dive bravely into the tidal waves,
sharp-beaked, but fail to disturb ocean's melody

I jump in to embrace the tides, paddling
slowly, floating atop the warm water,
only to be lifted up into a total wetness
for a good taste of the bitter, salty ocean

Drafted on the Florida Beaches with Virginia in 2005
Edited on August 8, 2017

沙灘上的卵石

在海邊拾起一塊卵石
光滑，石質，握力好
又看見一枚閃光的貝殼
半露半掩地埋在黃沙裡

卵石從我的手中滑落
我毫不猶豫地去拾
那片大海送來的貝殼
無意中，把卵石踩進沙裡

潮汐如千軍萬馬奔騰而至
我放下貝殼，好似一葉扁舟
停泊在沙灘上。我揮動雙臂
一步步地走向大海的深處

踏浪，蹦浪，當我和浪花一起升出水面的時候，
我吃驚地看見：海鷗在我頭頂上盤旋，頗有俯沖之勢
瞬間，我頓悟一個亞里斯多德靈感："散開！"
我發出鳥兒般歇斯底里的尖叫："我不是魚！"

中文2017年8月28日
Chinese poem August 28, 2017

A Pebble on the Beach

Picking up a pebble on the beach
smooth, stony, and a good grip
I see a shell, glittering in the sand
half-buried, half revealing

dropping the pebble, almost instantly
I seem to favour the shell from the sea
without giving a second thought,
when I step on the pebble, accidentally

tides rush in like galloping horses
I leave the shell to face up, like a tiny boat
mooring on the beach. Now swinging my arms
in the air, I wade into the depths of the sea

jumping, splashing, when I rise up with the waves,
surprised I see gulls hovering over my head, ready
to plunge. Suddenly, I hit upon an Aristotelian inspiration—
"Scatter!" I scream with avian hysteria, "I am not a fish!"

December 26, 2013
(At home on Boxing Day, pondering on causality)
Edited on August 11, Oct. 22, 2017

三葉草

春天的霧籠罩著安大略湖，春雨綿綿
濛濛雨簾的路旁，有一家花店
隱隱約約，我看見婷婷玉立的三葉草
就毫不猶豫地走進花店，買了兩盆春天

豪雨劈劈啪啪地下著
水珠從三葉草上滴下來
纖細的枝條彎下腰
我把春天捧進了家門

剛到我家的頭幾天
三葉草不再開花
嬌柔的小花骨朵
開始枯萎了

我給它們澆水
像下雨那樣
單日的早晨，雙日的晚上
三葉草合上了葉瓣
綠色和紫色的，好像
飛蛾合上翅膀
棲息在花盆裡
做起了蝴蝶夢

春天的霧，籠罩著安大略湖，
陽光常常破霧而出
三葉草在我的家裡
雙日的早上，單日的晚上
為我的身邊增添了快樂

一個星期日的清晨
無數白色和粉色的花朵
燦爛地綻放了！
美麗多姿的小花
舒展綠色和紫色的葉瓣
好像蝴蝶展開了翅膀

中文2017年8月28日
Chinese poem August 28, 2017

Shamrocks

Spring fog wraps up Lake Ontario
misty rain in large drops, hidden
behind the morning shower,
on the roadside—a floral shop

with a glimpse of delicate shamrocks
I rush into the store
to pick up two pots of spring
without a thought

pouring rain with spattering noise,
dripping from my shamrocks
their slim stocks bending low
I have brought spring home

in the next day or two
my shamrocks stop blooming
their fragile little flower buds
start to wither

I give them water, like raindrops,
on even days and odd nights
they fold up their leaves
green and burgundy, like moths
resting in the flower pots
having a butterfly dream

spring fog wraps up the lake
sunshine sometimes breaks out
the shamrocks live in my house
on odd days and even nights
a small happiness around

one Sunday morning
pink and white flowers
suddenly blooming aloud,
fresh, delicate, and cheerful
unfolding
their butterfly wings

First draft on March 18, 2016
Edited August 5, 2017

我是一顆星

我是一顆星
在邈邈的遠方
透過無邊的黑夜
送來我的光
當你看到一顆火花閃現
從目不可及的星雲
穿過厚厚的大氣層
千年萬載已經逝去

光陰荏苒
過去的十年
你瞇著雙眼
遙望夜空
尋找那顆眨眼的星
在邈邈的遠方
像磁鐵,
它的魔力
誘惑著你

夢中見到你的星
用雙手把她捧起
像蚌殼呵護著珍珠
五光十色
不再遙遠
不再分離

我是一顆星
在浩渺不可及的星雲
你的心臟激烈地跳動
青春的熱血奔湧
我跨越了銀河
十幾萬年前
今夜閃爍
你的星

中文2017年8月28日
Chinese poem August 28, 2017

Call Me a Star

I am a star
shining from afar . . . afar
through dark nights
sending you my light
from a distant nebula
when you see a little spark
shining through the thick atmosphere
hundred-thousand-years apart

in your ten-year past
you looked through the night sky
with squinty eyes, searching
for your blinking star
it seduces you with hope
like a magnet
its magical power
draws you

you dream of your star
to pick her up
in your cupped palms
like a pearl inside its shell
shining
no longer far
no longer apart

I am a star
an elusive star
in some nebula
your heart beats fast
with young blood
I crossed the Milky Way
a hundred thousand years ago
sparkling tonight
your star

Oct. 26, 2013
Edited August 10, 2017

樹上的蘋果

他把一個蘋果放在我的腳邊
他說，十年前他種下了這棵蘋果樹

我說，我從來不知道有這麼一棵樹
更不知道有人為我守護樹上的一個果子

他說，如今這個蘋果已經被摘下
是你，親手把它從地上拾起

我說，難道我就要接受合夥人的關係？
我從來沒有和你簽署過任何協議

他說，蘋果不是沙灘上的一塊卵石
也不是大海裡漂來的一枚貝殼

我好笑地問，難道我們之間不需要相互吸引？
他平靜地答，芸芸眾生遵循牛頓的萬有引力

我慎重地問，那麼"愛"到底是怎麼產生的？
你可以不讓你的蘋果從樹上掉下來！

"愛是精神火花碰撞的結果，"他的心火
已經點燃，臉色微紅，腼腆地娓娓道來——

"作為最高的精神境界，愛用一根無形的繩索
把兩個陌生人捆綁在一起，去超越自發性的局限"

中文2017年8月30日
Chinese poem August 30, 2017

An Apple on the Tree

He drops an apple at my feet, he says
ten years ago he planted the apple tree

I never knew there was such a tree, I respond,
nor someone was guarding a fruit on the tree for me.

Now that the apple has been plucked, he continues,
and you, who picked it up with your own hands

Did I, then, assume a partnership? I challenge him,
I have never signed an agreement with you.

An apple is not a pebble on the beach, he
argues, nor a piece of shell from the sea

But isn't there a need for temptation? I ask sarcastically.
On earth, he answers calmly, all abide by the law of gravity

How did personal interest happen to exist? Seriously, I ask,
And why didn't you keep your apple on the tree?

Love results from mental friction, he sparks, blushing
a little, his physicality starts to discharge its energy

At the highest spiritual level, he elaborates eloquently, love
ties up two strangers with an invisible cord to outlast spontaneity

December 27, 2013
(At home, tracing causality of love)
Edited August 11, 2017

小海鷗和蓮蓬子

有時
在黑暗的沉睡中
靈魂甦醒了
猶如一隻螢火蟲
振動著翅膀
不再畏懼
渴望發光

有時
在沉寂的密室裡
靈魂在躁動
像一顆蓮蓬子
釋放出微弱的呼吸
懷中的胚芽
渴望生髮

靈魂矗立
像小海鷗
從懸岩峭壁上
飛向蔚藍色的天空
"kittiwake，kittiwake！"
這是我的名字！
抖落幾片羽毛
帶著歡樂的疼痛
幾聲啁啾，發出內心的呼號
告別平庸，飛出生命的不朽

靈魂喜慶
像萌芽的蓮蓬子
為了滿塘的碧綠
綻放出柔美的粉紅
陽光下璀璨
月光裡靜立
風雨中搖曳
雖根植腐朽
超脫的氣質
純潔無垢

中文2017年8月30日
Chinese poem August 30, 2017

Kittiwakes and Lotus Seeds

Sometimes
the soul wakes up
from a dark slumber
flicking its wings
like a firebug
fearing no more
to make a light

Sometimes
the soul stirs
from its quiescent chamber
releasing a tiny breath
like a lotus seed
an embryo
destined to sprout

the soul rises up
like a kittiwake
flashing its wings on a cliff edge
soaring up to the blue sky
"kittiwake, kittiwake!
never forget my name!"
a few feathers dropping,
chirping, a heartfelt scream:
leaving a ghastly life
taking an immortal flight

the soul celebrates
like a lotus seed
dreaming to bloom—
the most delicate pink,
its green leaves covering up
the entire lotus pond:
brilliant in the sun,
tranquil under the moon,
strenuous in the rain,
with roots in mortal decay,
its proud soul
above the sludge
untainted

January 10, 2014;
August 11, 2017

Note on the poem:

Two days before the scheduled mediation for my litigation, I remembered kittiwakes, a species of small gulls in the Arctic. The birds, surviving on ragged rocks, with apparently incredible courage fly straight up towards the sky and bright light. I also have immense admiration for the beautiful lotus flowers, rooted in the quagmire of the West Lake in Hangzhou, my hometown and birthplace. The lotus flower has long become a symbol in classic Chinese art and poetry for its untainted spiritual quality.

January 10, 2014
August 11, 2017

題記：

在既定的法律調解的前兩天，我想起北冰洋上一種體型極小的三趾鷗。這種鳥類生存海洋中礁石的懸崖峭壁上，似乎擁有令人難以置信的勇氣，它們幾乎是直線地飛向天空和光明。我又想起老家和出生地杭州西湖裡的荷花，生長在沼澤汙泥裡，卻不被污垢的環境所改變。在中國古典詩詞繪畫裡，蓮花的品質早已成為精神和倫理的象徵。

2014年1月10日初稿
2017年8月11日修改

Song of Hope
希望之歌

the soul throbs

searching for hope . . .

靈魂在顫抖

尋求希望——

難民申請人

律師費吞食了你的銀行賬戶
血汗工廠餵不飽飢餓的狗
你拒絕接受政府的資助
救濟金會讓你在法庭上失去尊嚴

這片廣袤的土地是上帝的國度
藍天下的自由屬於所有的人
白雲變成雪花飄灑
回落大地江河湖泊

伸出你謙卑的雙手吧
或許你會得到高山上的甘露
願上帝用慈悲憐憫對你裁判
尚知廉恥的人獲得人間大愛

中文2017年8月31日
Chinese poem August 31, 2017

A Refugee Claimant

Legal fees have swallowed your bank account
sweatshop labour can't feed the hungry dogs
but you chose to decline government handouts
a welfare recipient may lose the dignity to stand in court.

This vast land is God's country, offering
freedom to all under the blue sky
white clouds transform to snow and
fall back on the land and the river

You may stretch out your humble hands
to receive mountain dews for those humiliated,
God may temper your hearing with mercy
granting you divine love with the judgment

Noted while waiting with a refugee claimant
in his lawyer's office, Nov. 12, 2012.

Draft completed February 7, 2013.
Edited August 11, 2017

難民申請人入冷宮

等待
彷彿被放置在擔架上
停放在醫院急診室的走道裡
無耐的等待，急促的心跳，劇烈的胸痛
窒息感，瀕臨死亡，無人關注……

死緩般的等待
一年，兩年， 三年，四年
已經進入了第五個年頭了
懸而未決，生死難定
腳下沒有一寸合法權

他是一個沒有身份的人
在加拿大，被長期打入冷宮
劇烈的疼痛變得麻木
流血的心，早已結上疤痕
仍然徹夜難眠，恐懼警察敲門

夢魘纏身，心急氣短
猶如一條絞索套住頸項
一個難民申請人，即
一個不值得信任的人。
如此， 政府部門批文
等待被發落

在他的聽證會上
一張嚴厲的臉坐在高處
領取高薪，法官貌似上帝
凌駕於一個沒有身份的人
沒有公民參於，不受社會監督

法官在挑戰他的大腦，期待
他的回答類似谷歌搜索引擎
"耶穌基督的祖母是誰？"
"耶穌基督出生前在什麼地方？"

A Refugee Claimant in Limbo

waiting, like someone left on a stretcher
in the hallway of a hospital emergency
with racing heartbeat, severe chest pain,
suffocating, dying, unattended . . .

dying a slow death, one year, two years,
three years, four years, and now
into the fifth year, living in suspension,
dying in suspension, without
a legal square foot under his feet

a stateless person in Canada,
he lives in a limbo, his acute pain
became numb, his bleeding heart
has scarred, but his insomnia worsens each night,
by the paranoia fear of police knocking on his door

nightmares, gasping for air, a noose
around his neck, pending deportation
for the untrustworthy refugee claimant,
sur place, penned by the Refugee Board

at his hearing, a stern face sitting up high,
a well-paid job, the judge looks like God,
dominating this stateless man
sheltered from public scrutiny

the judge picks the brain of the refugee claimant,
expecting answers from Google Search Engine
"Who is the grandmother of Jesus Christ?
Where was Jesus Christ before he was born?"

朦朧中他記得祖母死於飢餓，1959年
早春，給孫子留下家裡最後一個紅薯
耶穌有個慈愛的父，他也有個慈愛的父
他的父親死於突發性心臟病，發生在
武警闖進入他家的大門之後

他心甘情願為追求自由而死，然而
死亡的卻是他的父親，一顆慈愛的心
父親的心血管被恐懼衝破，大出血而亡
沒有見到兒子，無人為他的亡靈祈禱

嚴厲的法官再次拉下臉，向他提問：
“基督出生前在什麼地方，他死後又去了什麼地方？”
他回答，“耶穌出生前， 在聖母瑪麗亞的肚子裡。
死後，他復活了，他的肉體消失了。”

“你不是一個正宗的基督教徒！”
嚴厲的臉下了結論，氣憤地宣布。
他沒有完全聽懂她的話，
他真誠地相信，信仰猶如一粒芥菜籽

如果，上帝面前人人平等
那麼，他也想給她兩個謎語：
一個針尖上能站立多少個天使？
一粒芥菜籽什麼時候長成大樹？

中文初稿2017年11月
Chinese poem drafted November 2017

he vaguely remembers his Grandmother, in 1959
she died of starvation, leaving the last yam for him.
Jesus had a loving Father, so did he, but his father died of
a heart attack, when armed policemen rushed into the apartment

he was prepared to die in pursuit of freedom, but instead,
his father died for him with a broken heart, his artery
burst open with too much fear, he bled to death, without
seeing his son, nor anyone else to cross his heart

the stern-faced judge asks him again,
"Where was Christ before he was born and
after his death?" He answers logically, "In his mother
Mary's womb before Jesus was born, and after death,
he was resurrected, so his body disappeared."

"You are NOT a genuine Christian!"
furiously, the stern face declares.
he can't understand why the judge was annoyed,
bona fides, he believes faith is a mustard seed

if all people are equal in front of God,
he would like to give her a couple of riddles:
How many angels can fit on the head of a pin?
When does a mustard seed grow into a tree?

First draft in spring, 2013
after sitting in a refugee hearing.
Finished on Oct. 31, Halloween, 2017

不容剝奪的權利

加拿大的沃土
大地母親的懷抱
孕育了土著人部落群
和聖潔的甜煙草

從世界的天涯海角
來了成千上萬的尋夢人
飢腸轆轆，攜兒帶女，男女老少
他們是天災人禍的倖存者
逃離強暴的受難者
持不同政見，捍衛正義的勇士們
他們踏上了漫長的征途， 前赴後繼
去追求一個生存理念
自由和平等

靈魂因人性而搏動
男人和女人創造了歷史
不畏艱險，不惜生靈塗炭，視死如歸
在我們共同的記憶裡
迴響著歲月的腳步
悲壯而沉重
無法忘卻

在孩子們的雙眸裡
我們目睹了一代代人的期盼
天地賦予人類的基本權利
如同陽光、空氣、水

Inalienable Rights

Mother Earth nourishes
sacred sweet grass
for the native peoples
on the rich land of Canada

From far corners of the earth, arriving
millions of dream seekers—
men, women, families with children—
survivors of famine and starvation
victims escaping war and oppression
dissidents fighting for justice
all embarked on the long journey
for the innate values, seeking
freedom and equality

The soul throbs to its humanity
men and women made history
risking their lives,
millions of sacrifices,
in our collective memory
footsteps of the past
heavy and painful,
unforgettable

In the eyes of our children,
generation after generation,
we witness the same expectation
the innate values
of human existence
like water and air
like sunshine

人性是個協定
是我們和大地母親的簽約
從出生到死亡
根植在我們的命運中
跳動在每個人的脈搏裡
在呼吸的節奏裡延續
在共同的理想中傳承
不可剝奪的權利
人類最高的精神境界

當土著人把點燃的甜煙草
放在我們的手中傳遞
當陽光射進我們心靈的角落
我們不再猶豫向陌生人伸出雙手
讓愛和信任去改變人類
用自信和勇氣
去擁抱不同的族裔和人群
自由、平等、尊嚴
是人類的基本權利

讓我們登上"希望之塔"
頭頂藍天，手觸白雲
去聆聽《希望之歌》
自由的鐘聲在風中敲響
樹木發出低沉的共鳴
遍地野花綻放，一望無際大草原
向著遠方滾滾而去
我們慶祝，我們捍衛
不容剝奪的人權
如同陽光空氣水

中文2014年5月5日
Chinese version May 5, 2014

Humanity is the treaty
we signed with Mother Earth
from birth to death
imprinted in our destiny
drumming in our blood
renewed on our breath
the inalienable rights
highest spiritual realm

When native peoples pass smoking sweet grass to us,
when sunshine reaches the corners of our hearts,
we hesitate no more to stretch our hands to strangers
with confidence and courage
we embrace diversities
let love and trust transform humanity
for freedom, equality and dignity

Let's climb the Tower of Hope
under the blue sky,
to touch white clouds
listen to the Song of Hope,
the bell is ringing in the wind
trees and leaves are rustling
wild flowers blooming
prairie grassland unrolling
to honour and to defend
the inalienable human rights
like water and air
like sunshine

April 12, 2014 first drafted;
July 20, 2019 rewritten in France

希望之歌[1]

——歌詞為慶祝加拿大人權博物館落成典禮而作，加拿大作曲家何啟榮（Vincent Ho）的交響樂章《尾聲曲：希望之歌》。 2015 年2月27日，溫尼泊交響樂團世界首演，客串女高音Lara Ciekiewicz。

希望——
靈魂在顫抖
尋求希望——

漫漫的征途
探索真理的道路
自由、平等
像空氣和水
像陽光
人類共享

希望——
讓靈魂甦醒
我們改變歷史
用愛和信任
去分享共同的夢
以自信和勇氣
我們緊密擁抱
鐘聲響起
帶來希望

[敲鐘，鐘聲迴盪……]

鮮花盛開了
我們祭奠
我們捍衛
自由、平等
像空氣和水
像陽光
人類共享

1 https://vinceho.com/project/postlude-song-of-hope/ 上網讀評論，聽交響樂。

Song of Hope[2]

Vocal lyrics for the symphony *Postlude: Song of Hope*, composed by Vincent Ho to celebrate the opening of the Canadian Museum for Human Rights. World premiered by Lara Ciekiewicz (soprano) and the Winnipeg Symphony Orchestral, February 27, 2015.

Hope . . .
the soul throbs
searching for hope . . .

such a long journey
to seek the truth
freedom and equality
like water and air
like sunshine
universal
for all

Hope . . .
the soul awakens
we change history

with love and trust
we share our dreams
with pride and courage
we embrace each other
the bell is ringing with hope

[bell ringing]

flowers are blooming
we honour and defend
freedom and equality
like water and air
like sunshine
universal
for all

Finalized on May 27, 2014

---

2 https://vinceho.com/project/postlude-song-of-hope/ Log on to read the review and listen to the symphony.

Here and Now
此時此地

tasting my breath
there is salt in my life
品嚐了呼吸
我的生命裡有鹽

雨夜即興亨利家

——獻給參加2015年亞裔文化月的藝術家和志願者

音符在飛舞
曲譜生疏
一曲古老的音樂
來自遙遠的疆土
一條大河叫恆河

它史詩般的經歷
無須用擴音器
一架古色古香的風琴
在Gauri的手指下
一起一伏，起起伏伏
像老人的胸脯
呼出經典的印度樂曲
引領我的思緒起飛
去追尋你的世紀滄桑

亨利遞給我一支碩大的毛筆
使我想起童年，往事歷歷在目
學習書法之前
我們曾寫過大字報
當文化大革命的風暴
橫掃傳統華夏的文化瑰寶

幽怨的印度民間古曲
穿越時空的迷霧
融入電吉他的旋律
傳出了中國稀世古琴的聲音
跨越四千年，在二十一世紀復生
悠然的禪意，天籟之音
緩緩地融入了當代爵士樂
和擴音器連接在一起

Improvisation at Henry's Home on a Rainy Night

—Dedicated to the artists and volunteers of 2015 Asian Heritage Month

music flying
notes unknown
an ancient tune
from a remote continent
a river called the Ganges

its epic journey
needs no amplifiers
an antique harmonium
heaves up and down,
like an old man's lungs
exhaling a classic tune,
taking my mind with it
to search for yours,
vicissitudes of centuries

Henry passes me a large Chinese paintbrush
reminding me of some childhood memories
before learning calligraphy, we wrote
big posters to cover the streets
Cultural Revolution waged a war
against traditional Chinese culture:
its treasures and relics

time-travelling
through the foggy eras
soft Hindu music merges into
the electric guitar, out flowing
another ancient tune, Chinese *Guqin*,
spinning four millennia,
reborn in the 21st century
its well-paced cadence, clear narrative,
as if from the clouds, remote and spiritual,
jams with contemporary jazz
on the amplifiers

此時此刻
雷聲滾滾
由遠而近
又聞擊鼓聲聲
那是我們的心律
墨汁飛濺，猶如大雨降臨
英語詩句在宣紙上鋪開
彷佛雨後叢生的野草
出現在後院裡

粗黑的筆墨線條
幼稚而拙劣
我們的腳印
印章般地
留在宣紙上

亨利舉起
一瓶橙色的丙烯
朝著我們即興創作的拼圖
激情地潑灑
是水，又是火
頃刻之間
融為一體

2015年6月28日晚，在藝術家和朋友們的聚會上：
Gauri Guha，劉宇衡，何家強，和趙廉
參與了一次多媒體即興藝術創作拼圖
這首詩是即興英語原創的譯稿。
中文2015年8月
Chinese poem August 2015

right now—
from a distance,
thunders roll in, muffling
the drumming of our heartbeats
when ink splashes like raindrops
verses in English start to grow
on the *xuan* paper
like wild weeds
in the backyard

right here—
our brushstrokes
thick and strong
childish and awkward
our footprints
on the *xuan* paper
our signatures

Henry picks up
a bottle of orange acrylic,
dashing it passionately
onto the collage
as water
like fire
instantly
a fusion

At the gathering of friends in the evening of June 28, 2015,
Gauri Guha, Brian Lau, Henry Ho, and Lien Chao participated in
a multimedia improvisation performance to create an art collage.
The English poem was originally created then and there.
Final completion on July 6, 2015
Edited Oct. 22, 2017

奔馳的太極馬

——為何家強當代繪畫作品《太極馬系列》而作 2018年多倫多《藝術家項目展》

黎明前的朦朧
月光散淡
他坐在逐漸隱去的月色裡
靜思瞑想，好似一株蓮
他在聆聽，晨曦降臨前的寂靜
等待新的一天破曉
太陽冉冉升起

他坐在土地上
身心接地氣
從自然界吸取生命需要的能量
陰陽兩大氣場循環達到和諧
他的內心充滿平和與安寧

太陽高照，他在工作室裡勞作
揮灑墨汁，水在宣紙上滾動
伴隨著心跳和擊鼓般的脈搏
太極馬誕生了：一個動與靜結合的載體
天人合一，給作者帶來深度的驚喜

生於馬年，他畫馬不知疲倦
然而他多次申明：馬並不是他繪畫的主題
他在繪製探索精神境界的心路歷程——
他目及的視野裡有一個終極的空靈

太極馬在他眼前跳躍
成為他世界裡的自然元素
像後院的樹木
山谷的溪流
溪流裡的岩石

Galloping Taiji Horses

—Inspired by Henry Ho's *Taiji Horse Series*, 2018 Artist Project Toronto

In the misty early dawn
he meditates, sitting down with
the waning moon, like a lotus plant
he listens to the stillness in twilight,
waiting for the day to break, the sun to rise

From the land he sits on, his body
and mind touching down, absorbing
life from the elements. While
Yin and *Yang* move towards universal harmony
he reaches an equilibrium and tranquility

When the sun is up, he works in the studio,
with ink and water, rhythm
of his heartbeat, pulses in his blood,
he creates Taiji horses—
high motion in tranquility, a deep joy in his heart

Himself, born in the Year of the Horse,
it never exhausts him painting horses. And yet
he declares: he is not painting horses as a subject.
He has been charting his own spiritual journey—
a visualization—toward the realm of the ultimate void

Taiji horses galloping on *xuan* paper,
they become the natural elements in his world:
like trees in his backyard, rocks in the stream
running down the valley

在風中奔馳，太極馬是風
馬鬃和馬尾騰飛助力
在雨中舞蹈，它們踢踏著馬蹄
打個響鼻，用振動波表達歡喜

無論多麼快樂，多麼興奮
在這片土地上，太極馬象徵著和平
猶如白雲永遠不會於飛鳥相撞
藍天之下，百川歸海而去

中文2018年3月8日
Chinese poem March 8, 2018

Charging into the wind, Taiji horses become
the wind, their mane and tail lifted.
Rushing into the storm, they dance with the rain,
their hooves kicking. Puffing out a deep breath
from the nostrils, a vibration of true happiness

However joyful, active and vibrant,
Taiji horses remain peaceful on this land
as white clouds will never collide with flying birds
under the blue sky, all streams flow towards the sea

February 4, 2018

我生命裡的鹽

亨利敲響了頌缽
發出清脆的金屬音
振動的聲波
帶著音階和音頻
厚實純正
漣漪般地在空中擴散
似一陣清風
觸摸我的肌膚
彷彿穿透三分

頌缽鳴唱
發出獨特的音響
彷彿在說停、停、停
奔騰的烈馬
萬般的思緒
多功能的大腦
匆匆的腳步
猶如飛轉的陀螺
放慢速度
此時此刻
暫停

傾聽我的心跳
心律是多少？
測量我的呼吸
肺活量的深度？
感知我的存在
什麼樣的節奏？

Salt in My Life

Henry hits the singing bowl
a vibrating sound
of metallic clarity
its music scales
pure and dense
like waves
spreading out
riding the air
like a gush of wind
touches my skin
almost penetrating
my being

the singing bowl rings
sending an audio signal
as if to say stop, stop, stop—
to the galloping horses,
all wandering thoughts,
multi-tasking minds,
rapid footsteps,
spinning tops

This is the signal
to slow down
to the ground
right now

Listen to my heartbeat
what's the ratio of speed?
record my breathing
the inhaling and exhaling
become aware of my existence
what's the rhythm?

我聽見亨利在吞嚥
他嚐到什麼味道？
我感到來自艾希理的能量
他沉浸於內心的靜寂
關注當下的片刻，練就了
一日多次打坐的功底

腦海裡有個影像：
頌缽鳴響
正襟危坐
置放在亨利緊握的手側
他的手臂懸空
呼吸輕鬆

此刻，
靜聽自己的呼吸
我的眼眶濕潤了
地球的萬有引力
使我控制不住淚水

兩顆滾圓的淚滴
像大海的珍珠
從我的臉頰上滾下來
砸在腳邊的地上

品嚐了呼吸
我生命裡有鹽

頌缽裡沒有任何東西
空是最終的目的
發出純粹的金屬聲
表達完美無瑕的存在

中文2017年11月17日
Chinese poem November 17, 2017

I hear Henry swallowing
what does he taste right now?
I sense energy coming from Ashley
he stays within stillness, focusing on
the moment, his daily interval meditation

My mind's eye holds an image:
the singing bowl sitting high
on top of Henry's folded hand
his arm suspended
his breath weightless

I want to hear my own breathing
but my eyes are getting wet
I can't hold back my tears
from the law of gravity

Two perfect drops of tears
like pearls from the sea
rolling down my cheeks
hitting the ground at my feet

Tasting my breath
there is salt in my life

Nothing inside the singing bowl
emptiness is its ultimate goal
its metallic sound, pure and intense,
manifests a perfect existence

Tuesday, Oct. 25, 2016
Edited August 13, 2017

Awakening the Land within Us

A Multimedia Poetic Stage Performance

喚醒我們心中的土地

多媒體詩歌表演劇

Text written by Lien Chao
Original video footage and production by Henry Ho
Music improvisation and production by Brian Lau

詩歌劇本：趙廉
視屏攝影/製作： 何家強
即興音樂創作表演： 劉宇衡

舞台佈置

【舞台中心的地面上覆蓋著一大張矩形的圖紙，紙上可見加拿大地圖的輪廓；在紙的四角，豎立著四個高度不等（20—28英吋）的木樁(4x4英吋)，象徵東南西北，每個木樁頂上放置一個頌缽。舞台中央的地圖上也有一個頌缽 。】

【備用工具箱：一張魚網、丙烯水質色彩：紅、黃、綠和墨汁， 數支特大號毛筆， 一台3D手提投影機。】

【演出人員：2 位演員，1位朗誦者，1位音樂人】

【演出時間：22-25 分鐘】

【幕起】

【表演者A：站立於舞台的右後方，手持一枝碩大的中國畫毛筆，瞑想】

【表演者B：舞台中央的地圖上，坐姿，瞑想，面前有一個頌缽】

【朗誦者：站立於舞台的右前方的講台後面】

【音樂伴奏：位於舞台的左後方， 坐姿，身邊是樂器和音響系統 】

【燈光漸暗】

【舞台背景牆： 視頻A+音樂#1，30秒】

【音樂#1：“藍天白雲”主旋律，表達自由、希望和理想 】

【視頻A：典型的加拿大風光：落基山脈、五大湖泊、草原、農田和野花，加拿大鴻雁飛過天空，成群的太平洋鮭魚回游，加拿大國家電視塔，城市景觀，人群在街道上行走】

Installation on the stage

[A large piece of rectangular paper covers the center of the stage; on the paper, an outline of a Canadian map is visible; at the four corners of the paper, four wooden poles (4"x4") of different heights (20"-28") are erected; a singing bowl is placed on top of each pole.]

[Inside a tool box on the floor: a loose fish net, tempera colour of green, red, and yellow, Chinese ink, a few large paint brushes, and a portable 3D projector]

[Total participants in the performance: 2 performers, 1 narrator, and 1 musician]

[Duration of the performance: 22 – 25 minutes]

[Curtain Time]

[Performer A: stands at far-right-back spot of the stage holding a huge Chinese paint brush, meditating]

[Performer B: sits at the centre stage on the map, meditating, a singing bowl in front of him]

[Narrator: stands behind the podium on the far-right-front corner of the stage]

[Musician: sits on the far-left-back position of the stage with the instruments and sound system]

[Lights dimming]

[Stage background: Start Video A + Music #1; 30 seconds]

[Music #1: the melody of "Blue Sky, White Clouds" expressing freedom, hope, and dream.]

[Video A: typical Canadian landscapes, e.g. the Rockies, big lakes, prairies, farmland and wild flowers, showing Canada geese flying in formation, showing Pacific salmon swimming in the thousands, showing CN Tower, urban sceneries, showing large crowds of people walking, etc.]

第一幕：加拿大的土地和她的遺產

【音樂停，　視頻停，　燈光漸亮】
【朗誦者，聲音緩慢地，好像來自遥遠的時空】
【表演者A 進入舞台，緩緩地圍繞四根木樁走動，展示太極運動】

朗誦者：

加拿大——
我們的加拿大，
一個自豪的Iroquois身份——
16世紀以前
沿著聖勞倫斯河畔
45個原住民部落
驕傲地稱他們自己是
Kanatas

從那時起
這個自豪的Iroquois原住民身份
就成為這片土地的名字
加拿大的含義是
"村莊"
"定居"

【沉默，5秒鐘】
【音樂#1起】
【表演者A擊響第1個頌缽，環繞四根木樁，展示太極運動，　第1 圈】

朗誦者：

我們的加拿大土地
她是神聖的
她是完美的

【表演者A擊響第2個頌缽，繼續繞四根木樁，展示太極運動，　第2 圈】

朗誦者：

她滋養了我們
她撫育我們成長

Scene 1: Our Land of Canada and Her Heritage

[Music stops; video stops; lights gradually coming back]
[Narrator: speaks slowly as if from a remote time and place]
[Performer A: enters the stage; goes around the four poles, demonstrating Tai Chi movements]

Narrator:

Canada—
Our Land of Canada,
was a proud Iroquois word—
used by the First Nations
before the 16th century
along the St. Lawrence River
45 native tribal villages
called themselves
the *Kanatas*

since then
this proud Iroquois identity
has become the name of this land
Canada, stands for
"villages" and
"settlement."

[Silence, 5 seconds]
[Music #1 starts]
[Performer A: hits the 1st singing bowl, walks around the four poles with Tai Chi movements, the 1st circle]

Narrator:

Our land of Canada
She is sacred
She is perfect

[Performer A: hits the 2rd singing bowl, walks around the four poles with Tai Chi movements, the 2nd circle]

Narrator:

She is nourishing
She is nurturing

【表演者A擊響第3個頌缽，繼續繞四根木樁，展示太極運動，第3圈】

朗誦者：

她是安祥的
她是獨立的北疆

【表演者A擊響第4個頌缽，繼續繞四根木樁，展示太極運動，第4圈】

朗誦者：

她是一片沃土
有著無窮盡的資源
她與天地同在

【表演者A：走到表演者B身後，站立】
【表演者B：擊響面前的頌缽】
【音樂 #1：繼續“藍天白雲”的主旋律，15秒】

朗誦者：

在加拿大神聖的土地上
人法地，
地法天，
天法道，
我們稱道為——
偉大的母親

【舞台背景牆：視頻B +音樂#1：陽光明媚，藍天， 白雲，山脈，北方松林，30秒】
【燈光漸暗】

【表演者A：從工具箱裡拿起3D投影機】
【燈光漸亮】

朗誦者：

我們的加拿大土地
我們偉大的母親
撫育了千千萬萬的生命
原住民部落群
成千上萬的
移民、難民
落戶在加拿大的土地上
成為加拿大人

【表演者B：擊響面前的頌缽】

[Performer A: hits the 3rd singing bowl, walks around the four poles with Tai Chi movements, the 3rd circle]

Narrator:

She is serene
She is solitary

[Performer A: hits the 4th singing bowl, walks around the four poles with Tai Chi movements, the 4th circle]

Narrator:

She is fertile
She is infinite
She is eternally present

[Performer A: moves behind Performer B, standing still]
[Performer B: hits the singing bowl in front of him]
[Music #1: continues with the melody of Blue Sky, White Clouds, 15 seconds]

Narrator:

In our sacred land of Canada
Man follows the earth
Earth follows the universe
the universe follows the Way
we call the Way—
the Great Mother

[Stage background: Video B + Music #1: sunny, blue sky, white clouds, northern pines on the mountains, 30 seconds]
[Lights dimming]
[Performer A: goes to the utility box to pick up the 3D projector]
[Lights back on]

Narrator:

Our Land of Canada,
our Great Mother
gave birth to
ten thousand things

First Nations tribes
hundreds and thousands of
immigrants, refugees
settled on the land of Canada
to become Canadians

[Performer B: hits the singing bowl]

第二幕：個人拼搏

【音樂 #2：出現戲劇性的變化，強烈的節奏，造成緊張壓力感】

【表演者A：使用3D投影儀掃過舞台，刺激表演者B站起來】

【表演者B：追逐影子般的幻想，在舞台上夢遊般地移動著，時而跳躍撲捉，時而俯地尋找】

【燈光漸暗】

朗誦者：

但是，有時候
我們的日常生活
像跑步機上的小白鼠
被設定了違背意願的速度

有時候
我們生活在致命的困境裡
像一條被打撈出水的魚
徒勞地，在漁網裡掙扎

【音樂#3：單調地撥琴弦，重複簡單的節奏】
【演員B：追逐影子般的幻想，回到舞台的中心；筋疲力盡，磕磕絆絆，抓住地上魚網的邊緣，拉到腳邊，演員B 倒在舞台上，雙腳被魚網纏住】

【沉默：15秒】
【燈光逐漸亮起】

【舞台背景牆：視頻C：演員B 的內心糾葛和鬥爭。 屏幕上逐次出現一系列表達演員B內心情感的文字：恐懼……？焦慮……？憤怒……？妒忌……？仇恨……？挫折……？絕望……？30秒】

【音樂#4：繼續表現人物內心的痛苦掙扎，重複簡單的節奏】
【沉默：15秒】

朗誦者：

生命是一段漫長的征途
有時候，我們未能實現目標
我們尋找別的出路
等待泥漿沈澱，塵埃落土

Scene 2: Personal Struggles

[Music #2: dramatic changes, intensive rhythm, and harsh stressful tone]
[Performer A: uses the 3D projector to sweep across the stage, stimulates Performer B to rise on his feet]
[Performer B: chases shadowy illusions across the stage as if in a dream walk, jumping up to catch something, or crouching down to look for something, repeating the same movements]
[Lights dimming]

Narrator:

> but sometimes,
> our daily life
> like a mouse on a treadmill
> with the speed set against our will
>
> sometimes,
> life is a deadly plight
> like a fish out of water
> struggling in a fishnet
> with no luck to survive

[Music #3: plucking the strings, spacing out, creating a simple repetitive rhythm]
[Performer B: chasing shadowy illusions, returns to the centre of the stage; exhausted, stumbling, grabbing the edge of the fishnet, pulling it up, and falling down on the stage with his feet caught in the fishnet]
[Silence, 15 seconds]
[Lights: gradually back on]
[Stage background: Video C: showing Performer B's inner struggle; appearing on the screen, one by one, are expressions of emotional stress: Fear . . . ? Anxiety . . . ? Anger . . . ? Hatred . . . ? Jealousy . . . ? Frustration . . . ? Despair . . . ? 30 seconds]
[Music #4: continues to express inner struggle, gradually quiets down, silence, 15 seconds]

Narrator:

> life is a long journey,
> sometimes, we fail to reach our goals
> we look for alternatives, waiting for
> the mud to clear and dust to settle

【演員A：愛撫地為演員B 蓋上一大張透明塑料布】

【舞台背景：視頻D：顯示滂沱大雨，沖刷污垢，滋潤大地 】

【演員A：用他的大畫筆蘸著綠色的丙烯顏料，開始將綠色滴在演員 B身上的塑料布上】

【演員B：在塑料布下稍稍地動起來，首先把雙腳從魚網解脫出來，然後逐漸地坐起來】

【音樂#5：溫柔的音樂如春風，小鳥鳴叫，大地滋潤萬物。繼續到第二幕結束】

【演員A：繼續用綠色的丙烯酸顏色在塑料布上畫線條；滴下一些黃色和紅色的丙烯彩色點滴，直到塑料布的表面被春天的顏色所覆蓋】

朗誦者：

我們為什麼不停地競爭？
直到大多數人敗下陣來，
只有少數幾個人成功？

我們能不能停止相互攻擊？
用對自己的愛去愛我們的同胞？

我們為什麼不能更加快樂？
我們為什麼不能更加和平？

【音樂#5：溫柔的音樂如春風，小鳥鳴叫，大地滋潤萬物。繼續到第二幕結束】

【演員B：掙扎著想站起來，演員A伸出援助的手】

【演員B：緩緩地站了起來，抬起頭，雙手從身後拉起彩繪的塑料布，彷彿獲得了嶄新的翅膀，輕輕地舞動。】

【演員A+演員B把彩繪的塑料布展示給觀眾們看，彷彿是一幅繪畫作品，然後平放在舞台左前方的地上】

[Performer A: with tender care, drops a large piece of transparent plastic sheet over Performer B]

[Video D: Shows scenes of pouring rain, splashing, cleansing, and nourishing the land, 30 seconds]

[Performer A: dips his huge paintbrush in the acrylic paints, dripping green colour onto the plastic sheet over Performer B]

[Performer B: starts to stir under the plastic sheet, freeing his feet from the fishnet, gradually he sits up]

[Music #5: soothing spring music with birds chipping; the land nourishes all. Continue to the end of Scene 2]

[Performer A: continues to draw lines with green acrylic, then drips yellow and red acrylic onto the plastic sheet until it is covered with spring colours.]

Narrator:

> Why do we keep competing, until
> the few win, and the majority fail?
>
> Can we stop judging each other, and
> love fellow human beings like ourselves?
>
> Why can't we be happier, and why are we not more peaceful?

[Music #5: soothing spring music with birds chipping, the land nourishes all. Continues to the end of Scene 2]

[Performer B: struggles to stand up; Performer A: offers to help]

[Performer B: rises slowly, lifting up his head, pulling up the painted plastic sheet on his back with both hands as if a pair of new wings, flapping his new wings slowly a few times]

[Performer A and B: each holds up a top corner of the painted plastic sheet, showing it to the audience as if showing a piece of art, then laying it down on the front-left-side of the stage]

第三幕：尋找內心的和平

【沉默：15秒】
【表演者A和B：　站立，瞑想】
【音樂　#6：尋找內心的和平與寧靜】

朗誦者：

生活中應該有這樣的片刻
我們能丟下手中所有的工作

去聆聽——
聆聽勇敢的百靈鳥的歌聲

聆聽——
我們自己的心跳
在加拿大的土地上縱情地歌唱

我們的心裡有美麗的憧憬
那是偉大母親賦予的愛
跟隨自己的呼吸
去尋找內心的和平

【音樂#6：“尋找內心的和平”】

朗誦者：

吸氣——
呼出——
吸氣——
呼出——

【音樂#6：“尋找內心的和平”繼續】
【演員A：擊響頌缽】
【演員B：也擊響頌缽】

朗誦者：

平靜的心態將開啟心靈的大門
你會感到內心的安寧
一個更加清新的視野
將引領我們前行

【演員B：擊響頌缽】

Scene 3: Path to Find Inner Peace

[Silence: 15 seconds]
[Performer A and B: in standing meditation position]
[Music #6: looking for inner peace: 15 seconds]

Narrator:

There should be moments in life
when we can drop all the tasks

just listen—
listening to the songs of brave skylarks

listen to our own heartbeats
singing joyfully on the land of Canada

there is a beautiful landscape in all of us
bestowed by the Great Mother's love
follow our breathing
to find the inner peace

[Music #6: looking for the inner peace]

Narrator:

breathing in—
breathing out—

breathing in—
breathing out—

[Music #6: looking for of inner peace]
[Performer A: hits the singing bowl]
[Performer B: following Performer A, also hits the singing bowl]

Narrator:

when tranquility opens the door
stay within the stillness
an ever greater clarity
will descend
to enlighten
our vision

[Performer B: hits the singing bowl]

【舞台背景牆：視頻E：藍天，白雲，風吹，野花在風中搖曳，展現自由和生機， 30秒】

【音樂 #1：重複“藍天白雲“的主旋律，帶著深度的喜悅感 】

【演員A和B：做太極拳互動；緩慢地移動，稍停幾次，擺出雕塑般的二人造型。他們的互動表示內心的和平通常轉變為對他人的信任，和對我們共同擁有的世界的愛憐之心】

朗誦者：

回家吧
朋友們，回家了
像加拿大鴻雁翎隊
像太平洋鮭魚群
道的回歸
代代相傳

【演員 B：回到坐姿，瞑想】

【演員A：站在B的後面，瞑想】

【舞台背景牆：重複視頻A】

【音樂#1：持續到劇終】

朗誦者：

為了藍天、白雲
為了陽光、月光
為了雨水、雪花和冰霜
為了我們的子子孫孫
喚醒我們心中的土地
在加拿大神聖的土地上
讓我們和平幸福地
生存

【朗誦者和吉他伴奏者步入舞台，和兩位演員一起面向觀眾，演員B 擊響頌缽，在清晰的金屬聲波消散之前，全體向觀眾鞠躬致謝】

【劇終】

[Stage background: Video E: blue sky, white clouds, wind blowing, wild flowers swinging, showing freedom and vitality]
[Music #1: repeat the melody of Blue Sky, White Clouds with a sense of deeper joy]
[Performer A and B: show interactive Tai Chi movements; they move in a circle slowly, pausing several times when they pose for a sculptural duet]
[Their interaction suggests that inner peace usually transforms to trust for others and compassion for the world we share]

Narrator:

Come home
come home, friends
like Canada geese
like the Pacific salmon
passing down this heritage
return is the fundamental movement

[Performer B: moves back to sitting position, meditating]
[Performer A: stands behind B, meditating]
[Stage background: Video A: continues]
[Music #1: continues to the end]

Narrator:

for the blue sky, white clouds,
for sunshine and moonlight
for rain, snow, and ice
for our children's children
awaken the land within us
on the sacred land of Canada
let's we live with peace and joy

[Narrator and musician join the performers on the stage, facing the audience]
[Performer B: hits the singing bowl; while the metallic sound spread out to fade, all on the stage bow to the audience]

[The end]

觀眾參與活動
在加拿大的土地上添加我們的顏色

【表演者A+B】

B：　我們站在這張圖上，它象徵著我們加拿大的土地。地圖上有手繪的加拿大地貌輪廓，還有不同顏色的丙烯線條、色彩點、墨跡 、水滴、和我們的足跡，反映了加拿大多種族和多元文化的生存活動，使得我們的加拿大土地成為今天的現實。

A：　加拿大土地廣袤遼闊，她接受了一切，擁抱了所有。

B：　讓我們問自己：我們人類的靈魂是否能夠反映出這種偉大的精神？

A：現在我們邀請觀眾們自願到台上來，通過你們內心的反思，用畫筆為我們加拿大的土地增添自己的顏色。

謝謝大家的參與。

Acknowledgement致謝

- 《喚醒心中的土地》首演，亞裔文化月開幕式，多倫多市府大廳，2016年5月13日。
- 《喚醒心中的土地》修改版由約克大學人文專業學科學院贊助，應邀為《加拿大比較文學協會》2017年會演出，懷爾遜大學，2017年5月29日。
- 參與兩次演出的藝術家有：何家強（表演者A）、伍偉雄（表演者B）、趙廉（朗誦）、劉宇衡（音樂伴奏）、馮雪丹（舞台管理）。燈光和視屏由何家強藝術學校的學生志願者擔任。

An Audience Participation Activity
Adding Our Colour on the Land of Canada

[Performers A + B:]

B: This sheet of paper, on which we are now standing, represents our land of Canada. Within the outline of the Canadian map, there are acrylic smudges, colourful droplets, and our footprints. They reflect the human activities, colour and diversity that have made our land what it is.

A: Our Land of Canada is vast; it accepts all and embraces all.

B: Let's ask ourselves, can our human spirit reflect such grandeur?

A: We now invite you, the audience, to come onto the stage. You may reflect on the nature of your own heart and add your own colour to our great land of Canada.

Thank you for participating.

Acknowledgement

- *Premier performance of "Awakening the Land within Us" for the Opening Ceremony of Asian Heritage Month Festival was staged at the Toronto City Hall on Friday May 13, 2016.*
- *Upon invitation, a revised version of the script, sponsored by the Liberal Arts and Professional Studies Department of York University, was staged at Ryerson University for the 2017 Canadian Comparative Literature Association Congress on May 29, 2017.*
- *The following artists participated in both performances: Henry Ho (performer A), Ashley B. Poy (performer B), Lien Chao (narrator), Brian Lau (musician), and Flora Fung (stage manager). Henry Ho's private art students provided lighting and video management.*

附錄1：視頻錄像一覽

1. 視頻A：典型的加拿大風光：落基山脈、五大湖泊、草原、農田和野花，加拿大鴻雁飛過天空，成群的太平洋鮭魚回游，加拿大國家電視塔，城市景觀，人群在街道上行走。【30秒，第一幕，幕起】【重複；第三幕，劇終】

2. 視頻 B：陽光明媚，藍天， 白雲，山脈，北方松林。【30秒，第一幕】

3. 視屏C： 演員B 的內心糾葛鬥爭。 屏幕上逐次出現一系列表達演員B內心情感的文字：恐懼……？焦慮……？憤怒……？妒忌……？仇恨……？挫折……？絕望……？【30秒，第二幕】

4. 視頻D：滂沱大雨的情景和雨聲 【30秒，第二幕】

5. 視頻E：藍天，白雲，風吹，野花在風中搖曳，展現自由和生機【30 秒，第三幕】

附錄2： 即席音樂創作意向和效果

第一幕：
音樂 #1：主旋曲"藍天白雲"表達自由、希望和理想。

第二幕：
音樂 #2：戲劇性的變化，強烈的節奏，造成緊張壓力感。
音樂 #3：單調地撥琴弦，簡單重複的節奏感。
音樂 #4：繼續表現人物內心的痛苦掙扎，重複簡單的節奏。
音樂 #5：溫柔的音樂，如春風，小鳥鳴叫，大地滋潤萬物。

第三幕：
音樂 #6：尋找內心的和平與寧靜。
音樂 #1：劇終重複主旋曲"藍天白雲"帶著深度的喜悅感。

Appendix 1: A List of Video Footage

1. Video A:

Typical Canadian landscapes, e.g. the Rockies, five big lakes, the Prairies, farmland and wild flowers, showing Canada geese flying in formation, showing Pacific salmon swimming in the thousands, showing CN Tower, urban scenes, and large crowds of people walking, etc. [30 seconds, Scene 1, beginning] [Scene 3, ending]

2. Video B:

Sunny blue sky, white clouds, northern jack pines on the mountains. [30 seconds, Scene 1]

3. Video C:

Showing Performer B's inner struggle; appearing on the screen, one by one, are expressions of emotional stress: Fear . . . ? Anxiety . . . ? Anger . . . ? Hatred . . . ? Jealousy . . . ? Frustration . . . ? Despair . . . ? [30 seconds, Scene 2]

4. Video D:

Scenes of pouring rain, splashing sound, cleansing and nourishing the land. [30 seconds, Scene 2]

5. Video E:

Blue sky, white clouds, wind blows, wildflowers swinging, showing freedom and vitality. [30 seconds, Scene 3]

Appendix 2: Ideas & Effects for Music Improvisation

Scene 1/Music #1: the melody, "Blue Sky, White Clouds," expressing freedom, hope, and dream.

Scene 2/Music #2: dramatic changes, intensive rhythm, and harsh stressful tone.

Music #3: plucking the strings, spacing out, creating a repetitive rhythm.

Music #4: continues to express an inner struggle, gradually tuning the music down to silence.

Music #5: soothing spring music, birds chirping; the land nourishes all on earth.

Music #6: looking for inner peace.

Scene 3/Ending: repeat Music #1: the melody of "Blue Sky, White Clouds" with a sense of deeper joy.

跋：融合

在人生的道路上，我不時地寫下一些小詩； 我視它們為種子，一旦成為胚胎，就把它放回到生活的土壤裡去。這本新集子裡的詩歌最初創作於2005 – 2018年間。在等待生發的歲月裡，一些詩歌參與到我對人生的反思，和我一起成長，最終成為我人生道路上倖存的見證。

在創作和修改雙語詩歌的過程中，我經歷了兩種截然不同語言之間的長期對話和對其中敏感的文化內涵的感悟。重溫舊情舊景，我保存了有意義的記憶，或者平靜地接受了它們的存在。

回想起來，從1999年起，我開始用英、漢兩語寫詩，為我的雙語和雙重文化的加拿大身份發聲。在創作《楓溪情》(1999)和《切膚之痛》(2004)的過程中，我確認了自己的身份。這本新詩集沿著文化共享的方向繼續前行。

過去的十多年裡，我參與了"亞裔文化月"的年度慶祝活動，有機會和多位亞裔藝術家探討跨領域的藝術項目。在音樂、詩歌和視覺藝術領域裡，我們創作出了跨傳統學科的多元藝術作品。這些作品吸取了古老的中國智慧，結合加拿大本土歷史文化，採用當代藝術表現形式和手法，最終通過音樂會、藝術展覽、教學車間、和多媒體舞台表演等形式， 和廣大的民眾分享，為加拿大多元文化遺產增添色彩。

這本詩集包含七個章節。第一章"大地空靈曲"是一首遊記式敘述體長詩。 紀錄了我和幾位中學老同學在2014年清明節回到 70年代被下農村，接受體力勞動再教育的偏遠中國小村落。

詩集中部的五個章節來自人生各種經歷的啟迪：其中有珍貴的片刻、難忘的聚會、目睹親人面臨生死關頭的絕望。靈魂深處的反思或許是走出感情陷阱和精神叢林的一條出路，然而，我觀察到幾乎所有身陷囹圄的人，都不曾放棄過求生的希望和勇氣，而且不斷地用持久的記憶相互勉勵。

Epilogue: Fusion

In my life's journey, poems have been created from time to time. I treat them like seeds; once it becomes an embryo, I drop a poem back into the soil of my life to grow. The poems in this collection were originally created from 2005 to 2018. During the long wait, some continued to grow organically alongside my meditative reflections; hence they have become the surviving witnesses to my life.

In the process of writing and rewriting, I have been engaged in continuous dialogues with two totally different languages and their cultural nuances. Emotionally, by visualizing and reliving moments of the past, I have kept some memories meaningfully alive or peacefully reconciled with their presence.

Looking back, I started writing bilingual poems in 1999 in order to pronounce my bilingual and bicultural identity in Canada. With *Maples and the Stream* (1999) and *More Than Skin Deep* (2004), I confirmed this identity. This new collection follows the same purpose in cultural sharing.

As a participant in the annual Asian Heritage Month Festival for more than a decade, I had opportunities to explore inter-art projects with various professional Asian Canadian artists. Together we have created interdisciplinary art involving music, poetry and visual arts, enriched by ancient Chinese wisdom, while relating to Canadian history and culture, and embedded in contemporary art forms. We presented the final products through concerts, exhibitions, school workshops, and multimedia stage productions, adding to our multicultural Canadian heritage.

This collection contains seven chapters of bilingual poems, beginning with a long narrative poem, "Silence of the Wild Land," a poetic travelogue drafted in 2014 after taking a retrieving journey with my former schoolmates to a remote village in China, where we were sent for reeducation through physical labour in the 1970s.

Poems in the middle chapters were inspired by various human experiences, including unforgettable meetings and the helpless despair at losing loved ones. While soul-searching meditation may offer a way out of emotional traps and the mental jungle, I have observed that those who are caught in their shackles almost never stop seeking hope and courage by commemorating the past.

在詩集最後定稿的階段，我強烈地感到，近年來創作的多媒體詩歌表演劇也需要紙媒印刷才有可能再次亮相。於是我決定增加第七章，一部多媒體詩歌劇的完整手稿。英語原創是為了紀念加拿大建國150週年，2016和2017曾兩次在多倫多演出。於是我把英語原作翻譯/再創作成為一部完整的漢語劇本，歸入了這本新詩集。《喚醒我們心中的土地》向加拿大原住民部落和加拿大土地致敬致謝，引領觀眾們去反思當代人的生活方式，從而喚醒我們內心的和平。

總體而言，我希望在這本詩集裡營造一種詩意和文字的流動感。很多詩中容入了自然聲和音樂聲，其中有頌缽的金屬振動聲、悸動的心跳聲、機器的噪音、爆炸式的雷聲、落地的雨聲、可聞的寧靜、和永恆的沉默。通過多種聲音，不同的主題、語言風格、節奏變化、情感色調、和詩歌體裁的轉換，從敘述體長詩到抒情短詩到多元詩歌表演劇，我希望和讀者們分享《我生命裡的鹽》，也希望他們能夠從中獲得新的能量。

我決定一如既往地繼續使用中文繁體字，抵製傳統漢字書寫體和印刷字體不斷被侵蝕和消失。目前只有在香港和台灣，繁體漢字的功能性得到保護和傳承，一些海外中文紙媒也為此作出了貢獻。

我衷心感謝我的出版社Mawenzi House Publishers 對我的創作的支持和鼓勵。感謝我的親朋好友在詩集定稿的最後階段，認真地閱讀我的文稿並提出了寶貴的意見。其中有徐學清博士，詩友Patricia Rivera，文學詩歌愛好者我的妹夫徐寅生。感謝藝術家好友何家強為新書設計封面，女兒趙航對雙語文本及時的電腦支持。

我還要特別感謝安大略省藝術基金會對類似的雙語項目的資助，以維護少數民族族裔語言在加拿大的功能性。這本英漢雙語詩集的出版為近年來大批湧入加拿大的中國新移民提供了一本他們渴望的雙語文學作品。最後，我希望《我生命裡的鹽》能夠吸引加拿大和世界各地的英語和漢語讀者。

趙 廉
加拿大，多倫多
2019 秋

Chapter Seven dawned on me when finalizing the collection. I felt an urgent need to extend visibility through print to the multimedia-poetic-stage production; its original version was created for Canada 150 celebrations and staged in 2016 and 2017. I have translated and rewritten the English script with stage directions into Chinese for this collection. *Awakening the Land within Us* pays tributes to the First Nations peoples and the land of Canada, drawing the audience's attention to reflect on contemporary life. It aims to awaken the inner peace within us.

Overall, I have hoped to create a sense of poetic and textual fluidity in the collection. Many poems embrace natural sounds and music, including metallic vibration of the singing bowls, throbbing heartbeats, beeping devices, explosive thunderstorm, splashing raindrops, audible stillness, and eternal silence. With the various poetic devices I have used, such as different voices and subjects, rhythms and emotional tones, as well as by switching from the long narrative poem, to short lyric, and to multimedia stage performance, I hope the readers will feel energized when sharing *Salt in My Life*.

I have decided to continue using traditional Chinese characters for this new collection, as I did for the previous two collections. In this I am resisting the ongoing erosion and disappearance of the traditional written/print form of the Chinese language, which has been preserved only in Hong Kong and Taiwan, and by some overseas Chinese paper media.

I want to thank my publisher, Mawenzi House Publishers for their continuous support and encouragement of my writing. I thank my friends and relatives for reading the final manuscripts, and providing me with constructive comments. Among them are Dr Xueqing Xu, Patricia Rivera, and my brother-in-law Yingsheng Xu, a literary reader in China. Many thanks to fellow artist Henry Ho for designing the book cover, and to my daughter Avianna Chao for her timely digital support for the bilingual text.

My gratitude also goes to the Ontario Arts Council for its financial support for bilingual projects like this one, to sustain the functionality of minority heritage languages in Canada. The publication of this collection offers one new book to help quench the literary thirst of the multitude of Chinese immigrants in recent years. Finally, I hope *Salt in my Life* will appeal to them as well as others.

Lien Chao
Toronto, Canada
Fall 2019

Also by Lien Chao

The Chinese Knot and Other Stories (2008)
More Than Skin Deep, Bilingual Poetry (2004)
Strike the Wok: An Anthology of Contemporary Chinese Canadian Fiction (with Jim Wong Chu, 2003)
Tiger Girl (Hu Nü), Creative Memoir (2001)
Maples and the Stream, Bilingual Poetry (1999)
Beyond Silence: Chinese Canadian Literature in English (1997)